Scale Up Millionaire

HOW TO SELL YOUR WAY TO A FAST GROWTH, HIGH VALUE ENTERPRISE

Gordon McAlpine

I dedicate this book to entrepreneurs, wherever you may be in the world. By starting up a business and daring to dream you deserve huge respect. I hope that this book can help you to reach your goals and achieve your dreams.

RƎTHINK PRESS

First published in Great Britain 2017
by Rethink Press (www.rethinkpress.com)

Praise

'Successful entrepreneurs know how to dream big and hustle hard. Gordon is no different and with this hard-hitting book he grabs the bull by the horns to show you what you need to focus on to grow your sales rapidly. *Scale Up Millionaire* provides a pragmatic, proven, process on how to ensure that what you do every day is helping you to sell your vision and fund your future.'

Alan Kenny, General Manager, Mimecast

'Gordon has written the book I would have liked to write. This is a superb book about scaling up a business, being an entrepreneur and what it all means at the end of the day. Most people just don't understand the process to success – to find out how to achieve it, I would encourage anyone and everyone who is starting their business or is in business to read this book.'

Paul Oberschneider, entrepreneur and author

'This book will help you sell more than you thought possible. Gordon's had huge success himself following the principles you'll read. He's helped countless others have similar success through his pioneering sales club. But best of all: he knows how to break it down so anyone can understand, follow and ultimately master it. A revelation.'

Andy Bounds, award-winning sales consultant, best-selling author and creator of the Sales Video Club www.andyboundsonline.com

'Gordon's book is written from his extensive experience crafting sales strategies that result in multi-million pound revenues. So many tech companies in particular are exceptional at creating powerful products, however they let themselves and their investors down by not putting the same discipline into the sales process. Very few businesses survive long-term without an exceptional sales approach; the biggest brands in the world employ armies of sales people and spend millions on training them. Google, Facebook, LinkedIn, Oracle and Microsoft are all known for their exceptional sales training and development. This excellent book will help your enterprise sell more products and services.'

Daniel Priestley, best-selling business author and co-founder of Dent Global

'I really enjoyed this book. It offers both practical advice on scaling up, as well as much needed inspiration! Anyone motivated to grow their business will enjoy this book and find the proven process it outlines easy to understand and follow. Unlike other business books, *Scale Up Millionaire* offers a road map to growth which places sales at its heart. Gordon brings his sales experience and successes alive in this book, which will really help entrepreneurs scale and grow their businesses.'

Eleanor Shaw, Professor of Entrepreneurship, Head-Hunter Centre for Entrepreneurship, Strathclyde Business School, THE Business School of the Year 2017

'Of all the great business challenges, creating profitable, sustainable demand is the single biggest barrier to entrepreneurial success. In this great book, Gordon's expertise and engaging style combine to explain what works and, importantly, what doesn't. A must read for any growing business owner.'

Guy Rigby, Partner, Head of Entrepreneurial Services, Smith & Williamson

'As a CIO, I've spent most of my career on the 'buyer' side, purchasing technology solutions, and my experience is that the vast majority of vendors miss the mark with their sales approach. By contrast, Gordon is the consummate salesperson and in this compelling book you will find out why, learn what good 'selling' looks like and use his proven process to sell to potential customers in a way that they would like to be sold to. When you achieve that, you will make the sales you need to scale up at speed.'

Chris White, Chief Information Officer, Clyde & Co LLP

'*Scale Up Millionaire* is the book I wish I'd been able to read when I began my journey as a tech entrepreneur twenty-five years ago. My time is precious and so I love this book because it's easy to read, simple to understand and yet it has the power to inspire and transform your approach to sales. If you're ambitious to grow your business but have the slightest doubt that you can, you must read this.'

**Andrew Anderson, CEO, Celaton,
software entrepreneur and investor**

Foreword

I first met Gordon when he asked me to present at one of his sales seminars many years ago. I was struck by his very approachable and humble nature for such a successful entrepreneur.

One often thinks of sales people as extrovert and flamboyant, but in fact, as this book articulates, sales is every bit as much about listening, empathising and interaction as it is about proactive engagement.

I am a great advocate of removing the sense of fear from both our professional and private lives, as I describe in my book *Forget Strategy, Get Results* and Gordon hits the nail on the head when it comes to the impact the *fear of failure* has on our ability to be successful sales people.

Ultimately, great salesmanship is something we all need, whether we are formally in sales, or in any other sector or function of business. It's a way of life and this book guides us gently through the fundamental tools we need to develop, first and foremost a confident personality, along with being comfortable in one's own skin. But it also delivers powerful life lessons which can be applied to our personal lives.

As I articulate in my book *Live, Love, Work, Prosper*, the principle of work/life balance is ultimately an outdated concept, and true success at both can only be achieved by ambitious people with work/life *integration*. To that end, Gordon's book is also a book packed full of life skills. Reminding us of how to approach situations to get the best result for everyone, and not to be offended by setbacks, but to use them as valuable learning points for the future.

Scale Up Millionaire will give you the tools to be a successful entrepreneur, but the book is really about making people fall in love with you, what you do and who you are. And whether that is your team, your customers, or your friends and family, the same principles of listening, empathy, understanding needs and providing solutions always apply. Isn't that what we all aspire to in life? Isn't that what we want? To be loved? Of course it is.

You won't just be a better salesperson, you will be a better person for reading this book. Enjoy!

Michael Tobin OBE
Maverick, Entrepreneur, Philanthropist.
Author of *Forget Strategy, Get Results* (2014); *Live, Love, Work, Prosper* (2017)

Contents

Preface: Achieving The Dream   **15**

Introduction   **19**
Scale up through sales   21
Creating a special enterprise   23
Open your mind, commit to action and apply the process   28

Chapter 1: Proposition   **31**
Product reality check – is it good enough to sell?   32
World-class propositions from world-class companies   33
The Why – the emotional bit   35
The Value – the logical bit   36
The power of practice   38
Summary   41

Chapter 2: Passion and Founder Selling   **43**
Passion is a powerful sales tool   44
No excuses!   45
Three steps to getting good at founder selling   49
Three steps to key skills   49
Start your scale-up with passion and founder selling   53
Summary   54

Chapter 3: Sales Reality Check   **55**
Debunking the myths   57
Modern selling: your opportunity   63
Summary   64

Chapter 4: Pipeline   **65**
Creating your pipeline   66
Who are your target customers?   67
Niche focus   68
Focus on building your pipeline   70

Your pipeline at the core of your sales focus 75
Summary 77

Chapter 5: People 79

What will your sales culture look like? 80
Ten Top Tips for hiring your perfect team 85
Leadership – what kind of leader are you going to be? 87
Building the performance of your people 89
Summary 91

Chapter 6: Performance 1, Prepare for your Perfect Sales Meeting 93

Meetings with multiple decision makers 94
What do we mean by 'performance'? 95
Why would a prospect agree to meet with you? 96
Building a top sales meeting 97
Sales meeting model: SPQ 101
SPQ Model 102
Summary 103

Chapter 7: Performance 2, The First Half of the Meeting 105

Before you rush into the meeting 106
Quarter 1: Rapport 108
Quarter 2: Curiosity 113
Summary 119

Chapter 8: Performance 3, The Second Half of The Meeting 121

Quarter 3: Demonstration 122
Quarter 4: Progression 129
Summary 136

Chapter 9: Precision 139

What is precision? 140

Precision in scale-up sales 141

Precision makes the difference 150

Summary 151

Chapter 10: Time to Take Action **153**

Business is tough, so tough it out 155

You've got one chance – use it 157

Lead with your passion 158

Enjoy the journey 159

Know when it's time to exit 160

Just do it 161

Epilogue: The Secret Millionaire **163**

Acknowledgements **171**

The Author **175**

Achieving The Dream

DATCHET, NEAR WINDSOR

A sweltering July day turned into a balmy evening. My wife Claire dropped me off at Slough train station for the short trip to the solicitors' office in Reading. I was on my way to meet my business partner, Steve; if all went to plan we were due to sell our business that very evening. Claire kissed me goodbye and wished me the best of luck. I felt nervous, very excited, and in a bit of a daze. After almost ten years of growing our business, BigHand, our 'baby' had now grown up and was about to be adopted by new parents.

When we arrived at the solicitors' office, we met the buyers of our business – four of our current management team! They would be buying our business in a management buy-out, with financial backing from Lloyds Development Capital (LDC) and HSBC. But first we had to shuffle from room to room in a blur of 'official' meetings to make this deal legal. The final hurdle was an 'extraordinary board meeting', where a gaggle of serious-looking lawyers told us that we would now have to resign from our business to complete this deal.

This was the big moment; this was why we had toiled for thousands of hours, over almost ten years. We looked at each other and I said, 'Steve, I don't know about you, but I'm having second thoughts about selling this business. It's just so special, I'm not sure we should walk away at this stage…' The room went silent and you could have cut the atmosphere with a knife. Steve paused for a moment and then replied, 'Gordon, I think you're right; this is just too good to sell!' Once again, silence. Then one of the lawyers stammered, 'Oh my gosh, you cannot be serious…?' I paused for thought, looked him straight in the eye, and, with a big smile, said 'Don't worry, mate, we're just pulling your leg. Let's get on with it!' The poor guy didn't seem to see the funny side of it.

So that was it. We resigned around midnight; the other guys signed their purchase papers and the champagne corks popped. It all felt great – the ice cold Veuve, the taste of success, the relief, the emotion. After a quick glass, the new owners of BigHand hurried off as they had an early start looming, when they would have to break the news to the staff that Gordon and Steve were no longer, and that they were now the new bosses of BigHand.

Steve and I headed off with our advisors to the local pub, the Purple Turtle. It was almost closing time, so we had a couple of quick celebratory beers and then we waited for the first train, the 3.57am from Reading – no limo for us, the train would do just fine. I invited Steve back to my tiny cottage in Datchet to continue the celebrations. We arrived back as dawn was breaking and made a pot of tea – rock'n'roll! We sat out in the garden reminiscing about the good times we'd been through together and marvelling at our fantastic journey, and how lucky we were that our lives were now changed forever. Steve called his dad and I called my mum. Claire came down with our three-month-old baby Mia to congratulate us and made us bacon and egg rolls. I felt exhausted but happy.

After grabbing a few hours' sleep, I wondered what I should do today. This was the first day of the rest of my life. I was 38 years of age and had no idea what I was going to do next. Then I had a brainwave – I would go to the cash machine and check my bank balance. Bizarre as it may seem, as we went through the tortuous process of selling our business we sometimes forgot that eventually someone would pay us money for the privilege of buying it. It just didn't seem possible that after so many sacrifices, and always investing everything back into the business, we as the founders would finally make some real money. So I headed off to the village cash machine, and with trembling hands put in my card and pressed the balance key. The balance slip printed and I squinted at it through half-closed eyes. I swore out loud. It was true, the money had landed and I was now a successful entrepreneur with a life-changing chunk of money in my bank account.

So what did I do next? I defied all the sensible suggestions of family and friends to be prudent, take my time and gradually invest the money into savings accounts for a few months or years (how boring). Instead I decided to smell the roses and realise a dream that I had been working towards. The year before, Claire and I had got married in a hill-top village in Provence and I had vowed that if we ever managed to sell the business we would return and buy a beautiful villa in this special part of the world. I said 'Come on, Claire. You, me and Mia are going to the South of France and we'll come back when we've found our dream holiday home.' A month later we had found the one and the deal was done. Sipping a chilled glass of Provence rosé on our new terrace, overlooking the pool and the vista of mountains and pine forest below, I could hardly believe this had happened to me.

Claire kept reminding me how unbelievably hard we had worked to build such a great company from the ground up, but my feeling then, as it is today, was that we were and are just regular guys. There was nothing we did that marked us out as anything close to geniuses. We were honest, hard-working, ambitious young men who were determined to go about growing a business the right way. When we started out, we had no crystal-clear vision of what success looked like, but knew that we wanted to try to build a special small enterprise with a super-positive culture. We weren't sure which products we would focus on and we certainly hadn't written a sophisticated business plan. But I guess we must have made some good decisions, hired some great people, toughed it out and had a few slices of luck along the way!

We certainly didn't start with a magic formula, and I believe anyone could do what we did. We didn't know if we were going to succeed, but we always believed that we could. I hope that reading this book will help you to believe that you can achieve your dreams, whatever they may be. If you believe that, are prepared to work hard and keep striving to improve, you will give yourself every chance.

Introduction

*'Start-up is good but
scale-up is great.'*

SIR TOM HUNTER

We live in an entrepreneurial world. The decline of heavy industries, the shift towards service-based economies, the game-changing influence of the Internet and the range of digital tools available have resulted in more and more people starting up their own businesses and becoming entrepreneurs. Exciting times, with endless opportunities for those with the right ideas, the bravery, and the backing to start up a business. We continually hear success stories of entrepreneurs who within a handful of years have grown and monetised their businesses, amassing vast fortunes in the process. Facebook, LinkedIn, Snapchat, Tinder, Instagram, WhatsApp...the list goes on and on. So it must be easy, right?

The reality is that successes on this scale are rare, and are often the brainchild of 'geniuses' who just happen to ride the perfect wave, have some lucky breaks and sell at the right time. I don't think I'm a genius, and I suspect you don't think you're one either. Sadly, the success statistics for normal people like us are quite stark and paint a far less positive picture:

» 70% of start-ups never reach a turnover of £300,000 a year[1]

» only 1% of start-ups ever exceed £7.5 million in annual sales[2]

» 90% of business start-ups fail[3]

In the UK alone, 608,100 new businesses started in 2015.[4] But we know from the statistics that unfortunately the majority of these businesses will not succeed. The reality is that failure is the norm.

After championing 'start-up Britain' for many years, the British government has shifted the focus to 'scale-up'. In 2014 it commissioned entrepreneur and experienced business adviser Sherry Coutu CBE to investigate why businesses are failing to scale up (grow) and how this can be addressed. This excellent piece of research has been published in *The Scale Up Report*,[5] backed by numerous top-level government and business figures.

On the back of this, the Scale Up Institute has been founded to ensure that scale-up growth is at the heart of the UK's business focus in the coming years. Reid Hoffman, the founder of LinkedIn, said at the launch speech of the Institute, 'First-mover advantage doesn't go to the first company that launches, it goes to the first company that scales.'

1   Daniel Priestley, *Key Person of Influence,* Rethink Press 2014.
2   Ibid.
3   Neil Patel, *Forbes* magazine, 2015.
4   *Tech City News*
5   Sherry Coutu, *The Scale-up Report*, scaleupreport.org.

Scale up through sales

I've written this book to help you to buck the disappointing start-up and scale-up statistics. I'm going to set out clearly a proven, practical process, focused on selling your products effectively, to drive your business forward. This process should give you the tools and structure to enable you to scale up your entrepreneurial business successfully.

In fact, *The Scale-Up Report* specifically mentions the importance of sales as part of its six-point plan.[6] And with the Brexit vote, the challenge of increasing sales in home and overseas markets may become even more of a priority for ambitious entrepreneurs.

If you follow the process and get it spot on, over the next few years you could end up running a business making annual sales of several million pounds (with a healthy profit) and have the opportunity (if you want) to exit and personally become a scale-up millionaire.

But, in order to do that you will have to make sales (and plenty of them) to grow in a highly competitive world. If you can get your selling engine running smoothly, you will have every opportunity to be a successful entrepreneur.

Is this book going to help you?

Before we go any further, it's important that you know for sure whether it's worth your valuable time reading this book. So let's explore who this book is for and who this book is definitely not for...

---

6   Sherry Coutu, Chapter 7: 'Increasing customer sales at home and abroad', *The Scale-up Report*.

This book is for:

» entrepreneurs with a tangible technology product (or high value solution) that is ready to be sold at scale to other businesses;

» rising stars who are probably already achieving six or seven figure turnovers but are not sure how to rise faster and further;

» people who like the idea of an 'achievable dream' that could provide a life-changing bank balance on exit; and

» founders who are prepared to lead from the front and step up to sell their products with passion.

This book is not for:

» people who think they are the next Mark Zuckerberg, Elon Musk or Reid Hoffman, and feel they just need the right funding to make their big idea pay;

» entrepreneurs who believe their technology is destined to go viral and that they are destined to become billionaires;

» owners of service businesses who aren't prepared to productise and who believe that selling complex, bespoke solutions can make them their fortune; and

» businesses who believe this digital world means they don't have to actively *sell* their products to become successful, as that's all done through *marketing*.

What are you going to get out of this book?

I'm going to show you a practical route to get from a few hundred thousand pounds in sales every year or perhaps even into the millions, right up to a successful business consistently making multi-million pounds' worth of sales every year (and growing significantly), while showing a healthy profit.

Importantly, we will also explore how you can scale up with little or no investment, debt or loss of your precious equity. I strongly believe that, increasingly, the majority of start-ups get the focus wrong by raising money through funding, which they believe will automatically drive growth. But will invested money necessarily drive growth? It might drive growth if it is invested in pulling the right levers, but equally it might not and let's not forget that it has to be paid back at some stage.

In fact, Pizza Express founder and serial entrepreneur Luke Johnson echoed my thoughts in *The Sunday Times* when he described funding as over-rated:

> *'Raising lots of capital — sometimes it seems that an entrepreneur has arrived if his start-up has received bountiful funding from venture capitalists, even if it has modest revenues and makes large losses. Too much cash leads to waste and permits poor economic models to persist for much longer than they should.'* [7]

Like Luke, I'm not against investment per se, as everyone needs some seed/start-up capital, but funding is not necessarily a silver bullet for scaling up your enterprise.

Creating a special enterprise

We're also going to explore how to make your company special by staying true to a strong philosophy that enables you to:

» set things up so that clients and prospects fall in love with you, your product and your people, right from the start;

» build a business in your own image without ever having to compromise on your vision and values;

---

7   Luke Johnson, *The Sunday Times*, July 2016

» create a highly investable/sellable business because you've built it with a powerful, systematised sales engine;

» grow and exit (if that's your intention) on your own terms, and retain control and autonomy along the way; and

» sleep well without worries or pressures from venture capitalists (VCs) because you have the tools, knowledge and confidence to scale up your business organically.

How is my story relevant to successful scale-up?

Before we delve into the detail, I'm sure you're keen to know why you should listen to me! So let me share a bit about my business journey and why it has made me so passionate about scale-up through sales.

When Steve and I set up a technology company, BigHand, surprisingly we knew virtually nothing about technology! I was a 29-year-old sales and marketing guy armed with a few years' experience at Astra Zeneca and Steve was a chartered accountant who had been working at PepsiCo. But we both had a burning ambition to be successful. Our start-up capital was a few thousand pounds sitting in our personal savings accounts from our years in the corporate world. Our HQ was a small flat in Docklands, London. We recruited our first two members of staff into that flat, and moved the sofas out and the desks in. We promised ourselves that we would drive growth through sales and not through debt. We didn't like the idea of borrowing money or selling some of our equity to investors; that felt high risk to us.

Ten years after start-up, our passion and focus eventually paid off in a multi-million pound exit. We had become scale-up millionaires, and we had stayed true to our original promise – we had never borrowed any money from the bank or raised any funds from investors. In fact, we had done exactly what Luke Johnson described as being 'under-rated':

> 'Once upon a time retained earnings was the chief source of funding for most businesses. Internally generated surpluses were used to finance growth. This means equity does not have to be diluted.' [8]

We had created a strong, innovative product ('digital dictation' software to help law firms produce documents more efficiently) on a shoestring, but our 'surpluses' were generated through making sales. As a result, we did not have to dilute our equity during our journey. The success of our sales philosophy made me proud, as I was the sales director who put in the early hard yards of 'founder selling' by breaking down doors and closing enough deals to keep us afloat and moving forward. I then focused on recruiting great young people to build our perfect sales team and create a sales process that kept pace with the demands of a growing business. We started to make international sales and created a channel to penetrate the global legal market. But ultimately it was our home-grown sales people who made the business fly by hitting targets quarter after quarter, as well as having a lot of fun along the way! They were a bona fide high-performing sales team, and I'll always respect their contributions hugely.

After leaving BigHand, I wanted to do something completely different, but something that was meaningful and could make a difference to others. I had the idea of creating a unique organisation to help sales leaders improve the sales performance of their own teams. I knew that being a sales director could be a

8   Luke Johnson, *The Sunday Times*, July 2016

lonely, high-pressured role, with high expectations but often with little support.

So I founded the world's first membership club for sales leaders, The Sales Club. During this six-year journey, I met some truly inspiring people, both from our membership and among the speakers/mentors who provided support, ideas and inspiration to help our members scale up through sales. I'm very proud of the world-class, blue-chip organisations and fast-growth small and medium enterprises (SMEs) that we made a genuine difference to, and I personally learnt a huge amount about sales processes and techniques, and about what best practice in sales looks like. I exited The Sales Club earlier this year.

I'm now super-excited to be back focusing on the technology world, personally advising fast-growth entrepreneurial organisations on how to scale up through sales. As a Business Fellow at Strathclyde University Business School, and a Tech London Advocate, I'm also involved in inspiring and mentoring the next generation of entrepreneurs to take control of their own destiny in this exciting scale-up revolution.

I've now been in sales for more than 25 years, attended several thousand sales meetings both on my own and with colleagues, and I think it's fair to say that I've seen plenty of examples of the best and the worst of selling. I've also been an entrepreneur for 20 years and feel I have a good grasp of what entrepreneurial success looks like.

Before we move on, it's important to say that reading this book is no guarantee of success, as after all there are no guarantees in life! But I do believe that if you buy into this philosophy and practical process (and work incredibly hard) it should give you a fighting chance!

What could success look like?

I am convinced that being an entrepreneur is the best job in the world and the ideal way to create an exciting and meaningful career, as opposed to cruising along in third gear in a large, comfy organisation. But let's be honest, it's only really enjoyable if you're successful! And we know the stats show that the majority of entrepreneurs fail.

So my objective is to give you all the help possible to make sure you are one of the scale-up successes. I think of my journey as 'the achievable dream', because I honestly believe anyone with the right attitude can do what I have done and potentially achieve a whole lot more.

A lot of entrepreneurship can be trial and error, and one of my aims in writing this book is to give you an easy-to-use process that will cut down on the risks you need to take and the mistakes you might make. I genuinely believe that the principles I will share with you can help to make you a highly successful entrepreneur running a profitable, valuable business.

If you get it spot on, you could exit in a few years, benefiting from generous entrepreneurs' tax relief and make as much money personally in a relatively short blast (10 years or less) as the highest-flying lawyers or doctors make in their entire career (30 years or more). If you achieve that, it will be a life-changing moment, and one that will give you ultimate choice over how you live the rest of your life. Sounds fantastic, doesn't it?

Open your mind, commit to action and apply the process

So how are you going to achieve this success? Well, as we move through the book I'm going to examine systematically a scale-up process involving these key areas:

1. Identifying the key elements that you'll need to master selling and create a scale-up business that makes a real difference.

2. Converting your solid product into a compelling **proposition** that will equal those of the world's leading companies.

3. Dispelling common myths and fears about selling to give you a focused mindset for success.

4. Channelling your **passion** and using 'founder selling' to make the right, high-value sales.

5. Developing a strong sales **pipeline** to fuel sales growth consistently and create momentum.

6. Building and leading a world-class sales team, centred around positive, driven **people** who consistently smash their targets.

7. Creating a sales **performance** quarters (SPQ) model to ensure you and your team perform in every sales meeting, regardless of the level of pressure.

8. Maintaining **precision** is the final piece of the puzzle: this will allow you to strive for perfection and stay ahead of your competitors at all times.

6-Step Scale Up Process

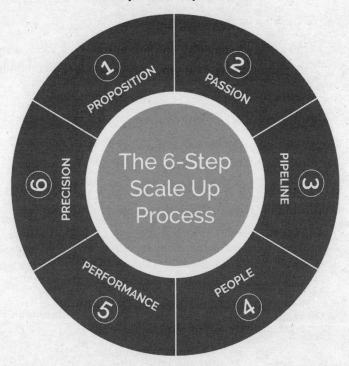

By the time you've finished this book, you'll understand the six Ps of successful scale-up, and you'll know how to use them in a simple, practical way to drive your business onwards and upwards (regardless of the challenges you meet along the way), towards your goal of becoming a scale-up millionaire.

At the end of each chapter there will be a brief summary of the key points to give you an easy-to-use reminder as you follow your exciting scale-up route.

Chapter 1

Proposition

*'Price is what you pay,
value is what you get.'*

WARREN BUFFETT

The value proposition is at the heart of everything you do to sell and scale up. It's the first, hugely important stage, which you need to get absolutely right. The value proposition can be quite a technical area of sales (and many books have been written on this topic), but I'm going to try to keep it nice and easy for you. By the time you've completed this chapter, you'll know how to build and refine your proposition in a practical, relevant way, so you're absolutely clear on what value you can bring to your potential clients.

To be able to sell your product effectively, you'll need to spend some quality time on this critical area. It's really about developing your ability to articulate confidently, in a relaxed, 'non-salesy' way, why people should buy your product.

Product reality check – is it good enough to sell?

It's important to mention that you do need to have a decent product in order to put together a strong value proposition. Your product does not have to be the next Pokémon Go, but as this book is focused on helping you scale up rather than start up, we'll assume you already have a strong, solid product.

If you're not making many sales with your current product despite having tried for some time, a revised proposition may help you, but it might also be time to look for a new product! There is no disgrace in that: our first product was only a springboard, and not the one that enabled us to scale up and sell our business.

Now for a quick product reality check – I believe you must meet these three criteria to have a chance of scale-up success:

1. Have a product which has the potential to deliver significant value to your target customers – to address their pain points and needs.

2. Be passionate about your product and the difference it makes. (You can have multiple products as long as they support the main product, but if you have a small sales team, multiple products can complicate the message and dilute the focus.)

3. Have a product that can be sold and delivered consistently without customisation. A bespoke product will undermine your sales activity because you'll be so busy customising that you will be distracted from your focus on sales, which in turn will hamper your potential to scale up.

So you passionately believe you have a good product and there appears to be a need for it, or at least evidence that people want to buy it, but sales growth is probably slower than you had hoped for. How do you make your proposition more compelling, so that it grabs people's attention every time they see it or every time you say it?

World-class propositions from world-class companies

What makes a great proposition? I think it's worth taking a quick look at some examples of how great companies communicate their propositions. It's unlikely a company will become one of the world's best without an exceptional proposition. These are three of my favourite tech businesses and it's no coincidence that I love their propositions too.

Apple

I've always been a fan of Apple and, whether you're a fan or not, it seems to me that their philosophy has stayed true to Steve Jobs's original vision:

> 'Everything we do, we believe in challenging the status quo. We believe in thinking differently. The way we challenge the status quo is by making our products beautifully designed, simple to use, and user friendly.'

Dropbox

Technology company Dropbox dedicates itself to producing simple, powerful products for people and businesses. When I read about the founder, Drew Houston, I was impressed by the fact that he appears to be a man on a mission, but he had to battle hard for quite some time to get people to believe in his technology. He also seems to be a man with soul who genuinely wants to make a difference:

> *'We create products that are easy to use and are built on trust. When people put their files on Dropbox, they can trust they're secure and their data is their own. Our users' privacy has always been our priority and it always will be.'*

I'm writing this book storing my files on Dropbox, and my positive customer experience matches their proposition, which shows they have got it spot on.

Slack

In a world where everyone seems to be constantly busy and time-poor, I love the simplicity of Slack's approach. They have created clever technology to help streamline conversations and communications within businesses and their proposition is quite simply:

> *'Be less busy.'*

Even their extended value proposition is simple and effective:

> *'We're on a mission to make your working life simpler, more effective and more pleasant.'*

The above examples are all very successful technology companies that have mastered the art of how to differentiate themselves from humdrum, run-of-the-mill businesses. But the most interesting point about their propositions is that they don't define in detail what they do or how they do it. Their propositions are all very simple, clear and inspiring, and they get your attention.

The Why – the emotional bit

So why are these propositions so effective? Well, all of these examples focus more on the reason they are in existence and their mission. They don't explain in detail what they do, or mention the specific benefits of their business and products. I've always believed that this is a very strong, non-salesy way to deliver your proposition when you first engage with prospects.

This concept of how to frame a winning proposition was developed by Simon Sinek in his best-selling business book *Start with Why* in 2011.[1] Sinek's core mantra is, 'People don't buy *what* you do, they buy *why* you do it.' He asks a challenging question that you, as an entrepreneur, should ask yourself:

> *'Do you know your* why*? The purpose, cause or belief that inspires you to do what you do?'*

Because The Sales Club was a new start-up and a fresh concept, my reasons for setting it up were very important and went something like this:

> *'Having been a sales director for 10 years, I passionately believe sales is the engine of any business and in order for that engine to perform well the sales leaders need expertise, ideas and support to be able to improve the performance of their sales teams. That's why I set up The Sales Club.'*

You'll notice that I focused on why I set up the organisation and didn't mention details of the features and benefits of the

---

1   Simon Sinek, *Start with Why: How great leaders inspire everyone to take action*, Portfolio Penguin 2011

product – plenty of time to explain that later, once I had got people's attention.

For you, as a small ambitious firm, starting with 'why' is possibly even more important than for these large firms. If you hit them too early in the conversation with 'here's how our product works...' and 'this is what our product does...' they will label you as just another sales person 'selling' to them with a long list of features and benefits.

Your potential customers will be keen to know your story: why you set up the business and why you created your product. If they buy into your story and your purpose in setting up your company, they will start buying into you emotionally. Creating an emotional connection is critical.

So if you already have a proposition, start thinking about whether it creates a big enough impression. If you don't have one, start thinking about what it should be, to inspire and excite your potential customers.

The Value – the logical bit

Now that you have a feel for what a good proposition looks like, the next stage is building the logical benefits and the value of using your product, as potential customers will need to hear about these at some stage.

Jot down these four key questions to ask yourself:

1. What does your product do? Focus on core benefits, not features.

2. What will happen for your prospects when they have it? Make sure everything you say is framed from the customer's viewpoint, not your viewpoint.

3. What will happen if they don't have it? Most people have a fear of being left behind by their competitors – this is worth playing on!

4. What value will your product provide to your customers? Put a value on using your product in terms of money saved, money made, time saved, productivity gained etc. Your potential clients will expect this. Customer examples and testimonials are important to back up return on investment (ROI) data, but use examples relevant to the specific customer, otherwise it looks like namedropping.

The Why + The Value = Emotion + Logic

To summarise: in order for you and your team to sell successfully, buyers will need to feel that they have bought into your story emotionally and that they have also analysed your product and are clear on the logical benefits before they can be confident about investing in your product.

The answers to the questions you have asked yourself should have enabled you to draft a proposition with both

- » emotion (which creates desire), and
- » logic (which creates confidence).

Developing a crystal-clear proposition is not easy, so what you have come up with so far may well need some fine-tuning. But you will probably not be a million miles away, so don't be afraid to continue to tweak and refine the wording until you feel it is spot on.

You will know that you have got it right when saying it out loud makes you feel proud, passionate and confident – and the person you're saying it to should feel excited, energised and inspired.

The power of practice

I've attended and chaired many workshops and seminars over the years with senior sales people, sales leaders and CEOs. It never fails to amaze me that when top professionals are asked to stand up and explain what they do, they generally struggle.

It's never easy to do this in front of your peers, but to be successful you must be able to do this easily, impressively and consistently. I'm convinced the majority of business people rarely practise delivering their propositions – which is incredible, really, as a powerful proposition is at the heart of effective selling. But, as so often happens, complacency kicks in and people forget to practise the basics.

Matthew Syed, a former table tennis player, is a sports writer for *The Times*. He has spoken to The Sales Club members on this subject and has written a superb book about it. *Bounce – The Myth of Talent and the Power of Practice* is a great reality check for all businesses.[2] I'd encourage you to read it, as his philosophy of continual practice and improvement could become a key factor in the successful scale-up of your business.

Practise your proposition

As an aspiring entrepreneur, you need to be able to get this right when the pressure is on and you're standing in a big pitch with some huge potential clients. Your proposition must just roll off the tongue in a way that makes the audience sit up and think, 'That sounds really excellent; I'm seriously impressed by this company!'

2   Matthew Syed, *Bounce: The myth of talent and the power of practice,* Harper Perennial 2011

The way to ensure this happens for you and your team is to practise your proposition time and time again:

» involve yourself, your fellow directors, and your sales team;

» incorporate this type of exercise into your regular team meetings (your people won't like it to start with, as it will take them out of their comfort zones); and,

» to take it to an advanced level, interrupt people mid flow, throw in tricky objections, and generally be difficult!

Once you can all do it well in front of your peers (always the hardest people to sell to), everyone will enjoy these exercises and find it easier to perform in high-pressure sales situations.

This process enables you to perfect and test out the strength of your proposition, and also to build resilience, so that your people learn how to deal with the tough questions and challenges that will inevitably come out in the field.

Make your proposition a key sales priority

So, the first stage of your successful scale-up is to create, refine and practise your proposition until you feel it is bordering on perfection. Make no mistake – your proposition will be at the heart of your ability to sell effectively and scale up! Get this bit wrong and the entire process covered in the book will work less effectively; get this bit right and you will book more meetings, impress more prospects, and your deal conversion rate will start to rise.

It's also important to note that your proposition needs to evolve as your company evolves. To get into another layer of detail and take your proposition to an advanced level, I would recommend an excellent book written by a friend of mine, Cindy Barnes, with her co-authors: *Creating and Delivering your Value Proposition*.[3]

By revisiting and refreshing your proposition on a regular basis, you will attract and impress prospects, ensure that your clients see that you are evolving, and make sure that your people remain engaged and motivated. You should now understand stage one of your successful scale-up.

---

3   Cindy Barnes, Helen Blake and David Pinder, *Creating and Delivering Your Value Proposition: Managing customer experience for profit*, Kogan Page 2015.

Summary

» Product reality check - is your product strong enough to build into a sellable proposition?

» The Why – do you know your Why? If not, you need to articulate it.

» Value – jot down a short list of the benefits and the worth of your product from your clients' perspective.

» Create a simple, clear, inspiring proposition – combining the Why (emotion) and the Value (logic).

» Practise your proposition – so that your people always impress prospects, even under pressure.

Chapter 2
Passion and Founder Selling

"

'People with passion can change the world for the better.'

STEVE JOBS

Now that you've created and refined your proposition, what should you do next? Spend a few weeks writing a sophisticated business plan to conquer the world? Go looking for funding? Start recruiting your sales team?

Personally, I'd recommend none of the above, as they will delay your first sales! The last thing you want to do now is procrastinate or make excuses. Right now, you personally need to get out and start making some sales, as what your business needs most (to start scaling up) is sales revenue. You can personally control and drive those sales using a practical, powerful tool, 'founder selling', which we'll explore in this chapter.

Selling is the key to creating a sustainable, cost-effective, engine to drive your business forward and allow you to scale up. You need to step up to the plate and accept, as a founding director or CEO, that selling is your top priority and one that you must take responsibility for. If you've been reluctant to step up, this chapter will help. Or you may already be doing some founder selling, but even if you are, you can always improve the way you sell yourself and your business.

Passion is a powerful sales tool

The key reason you should get out there first and make the first sales is that you are the one with the passion. The very fact you've started up a business proves you have a vision, a dream, and loads of passion and drive. And potential clients will want to meet you and find out exactly why you're so passionate. But what exactly does passion mean? This great quote from Dave Kerpen, CEO of inc.com sums it up perfectly:

> *'Passion is the energy that keeps us going, that keeps us filled with meaning, and happiness, and excitement, and anticipation. Passion is a powerful force in accomplishing anything you set your mind to, and in experiencing work and life to the fullest extent possible. Ultimately, passion is the driving force behind success and happiness that allows us all to live better lives.'*

Sequoia Capital's Doug Leone spoke about the importance of passion for entrepreneurs at a recent conference. The legendary investor has backed Google, Airbnb, WhatsApp and hundreds of other entrepreneurial companies.

'What is the one quality all of the successful entrepreneurs share?' an audience member asked. 'They don't do it for the money,' Leone quickly responded. 'They're passionate about their mission.'

Their mission might be to disrupt a category; their mission might be to solve a problem they faced themselves; their mission might be to leave the world a better place; but in every case the mission is deeper and more meaningful than the product or service alone, and the mission creates the passion.

As an ambitious entrepreneur, if you can channel your passion in the right way, it will become a powerful sales tool to inspire people to buy your products and help to drive your business forward.

At this stage of your development, you may not know exactly how you are going to achieve your entrepreneurial dreams, but:

» you have a product;

» you have a proposition; and

» you have passion.

The good news is that these are all the ingredients you need to start making sales, driving growth and scaling up your business.

No excuses!

Before we explain more about using your passion when founder selling, let's step back for a moment and look at some potential challenges to how this can work for you. The reason I mention this is that I've met many founders and CEOs who don't think selling should be a key part of their role. You too may well have reservations about whether you should or can sell, so let's take a look at some of the common excuses to see why this attitude can be a barrier to successful scale-up and how to overcome it.

Excuse 1: I'm not a sales person

I didn't believe I could ever be a good sales person either, but having plunged into it accidentally, I would definitely say that selling has been the most significant factor in driving my career success. I hear this excuse all the time, but I strongly believe it's your job to sell. The problem often arises because beliefs about what selling actually is are often wrong. We'll explore and dispel some of the common myths in Chapter 3. Once you master selling, you will have greater control and confidence in your ability to grow a successful business. Selling is a key business skill that will make you a stronger entrepreneur.

Excuse 2: I'm the CEO; my job is to focus on strategy

Business doesn't exist without sales. Strategy without sales is meaningless. As the boss, you need to set an example. If you believe that your skill set lies elsewhere and have a co-founder, it is imperative that at least one of you is fully focused on sales. But if you are the CEO, you should spend as much time in front of clients and potential clients as you do in the office.

Excuse 3: I'll hire a sales person when we have more budget

Where do you think the budget comes from? Sales! You must realise that nobody you hire is going to have the same level of passion as you. Good sales people command a premium and until you start filling your bank account, you will not be able to afford anyone in your league. If you're looking for funding to drive your growth, you may also find that investors push back against their money being spent on star sales people.

Better to decide when and who you recruit from a position of strength. Also, if you haven't mastered sales yourself when you start recruiting a sales team, you won't be tuned in to your team. You can (and must) recruit and develop a sales team as you scale up – but it begins with you.

Excuse 4: I've already got a sales team, so sales is sorted

Even if you've already hired a sales director/manager and a small sales team, sales is never 'sorted' as you can always improve performance. Get back out there and sell your vision to prospects, customers, partners – in fact, anyone who is prepared to listen. Gain respect for yourself (and, as you grow, from your team) by making the most important element of a business – the ability to sell – your core skill. At my technology firm, I continued to sell (as well as lead the sales team) from day one right up to the day of my exit. Believe me, you will gain maximum respect from your staff if you lead from the front!

Excuse 5: I don't have the time to sell

Unless you're speaking to customers or serving customers you should always make time for selling. If you think that you don't have time, what are you doing? It's easy to fill our days emailing, firefighting, tweeting/posting and just generally keeping busy. But if you don't take the responsibility for driving sales you may find yourself with a nice office, cool brand, great processes, but little sales revenue, no profit and no business. Do you think Sir Richard Branson ever says to his team 'Sorry guys, I can't go to this event that could make our Virgin Galactic sales sky-rocket, I need to clear my inbox.'? The best of the best entrepreneurs always make time for selling!

Fear as a barrier

Looking at these potential excuses, it's fair to say that our excuses often mask our fears. I know it's hard to admit that you may have fears! But we are all scared of something and our fears about selling are likely to include fears of:

> » rejection: this is a primal fear but pointless. Rejection is not normally a reflection of you but a reflection of the fact you need to make some tweaks. Treat rejection as feedback and you will keep getting better – a sentiment echoed by Bill Gates when he said, 'Your most unhappy customers are your greatest source of learning';

> » humiliation: you don't have to be totally shameless but you do need to lighten up and not take mistakes or knock-backs personally – once again, they're lessons to reflect on and learn from; and

> » success: people don't like to admit to this fear, but it can often be a deep-rooted fear at the heart of your subconscious, because success can lead to hard work, hassle, raised expectations and, oddly, fear of failure when it comes to delivery.

Susan Jeffers describes the perfect, fearless mindset for entrepreneurs in the title of her excellent book as *Feel the Fear and Do It Anyway*.[1] You will have some fears; you are human after all! But be brave, get stuck into selling your vision, and they will quickly disappear.

---

1   Susan Jeffers, *Feel the Fear and Do It Anyway*, Vermilion 2011

Three steps to getting good at founder selling

So, founder selling is critical to your success. It all makes perfect sense, doesn't it? But you may still harbour some doubts about whether you can succeed at selling. You may feel that you are not a natural sales person. And you may not be, very few of us are… but my experience is that in the entrepreneurial world, if you have the right attitude and are prepared to give it a go, it is actually quite easy to learn the techniques and skills to become confident at selling.

I've always used this simple three-step process, which will help to focus you on the key skills for starting to make sales. You need to cover all three steps for this to be properly effective.

Three steps to key skills

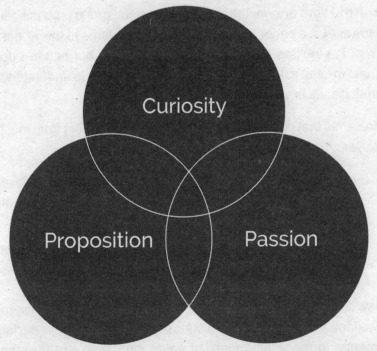

Curiosity

Curiosity is at the heart of good selling. If you can tap into your curiosity, you will sell well. So what exactly is curiosity? The dictionary definition is 'a strong desire to know or learn something'.

If we explore that in a sales context, curiosity means being genuinely interested in the person you are talking to. The easiest way to demonstrate curiosity is by asking questions and listening. It sounds simple, but few people do this well. And in the context of sales, it is critical to probe deeper, as this is where you will find out about people's needs and problems, which will allow you to offer your product as a potential solution.

When you attend a sales meeting, the chances are it's you who asked for the meeting, so the prospect will probably say 'so tell me more about your business' early on in the meeting. You could always answer the question with your strong proposition! However, it's better to turn the tables with words to this effect: 'Yes, I'm looking forward to explaining more, but before I do that I'm keen to know more about your company to understand specifically how we might be able to help you.'

Trust me, that curious response will gain you respect from most buyers, as human nature means that they will be:

» relieved that you have not launched into some 'salesy' sales pitch (reeling off a long list of dull features parrot-fashion); and

» flattered that you appear genuinely interested in them and their business.

We'll explore curiosity in more detail in Chapters 6–7, when we look at how you can use curiosity to maximise your performance in those all-important sales meetings. But for now, remember that the best sales people use curiosity, thought-fulness, reflection and effective listening to engage with and impress their clients.

Proposition

We explored the importance of your proposition and how to put a strong proposition together in Chapter 1. Your story is what should intrigue your potential client, and as they are expecting you to sell them something, they are likely to want to hear your proposition (your 'elevator pitch') early in the meeting. This is why the practice sessions mentioned in the last chapter are so important, as your response must sound genuine, authentic and inspirational. After all, it was your idea to create this busi-ness and this product, so the prospect needs to understand why you have done this.

Passion

Having laid the foundations with curious questions and an impressive proposition, you can then differentiate yourself from the competition by pumping up your prospect with passion. But don't forget that curiosity is the foundation stone for building a relationship, which you can then capitalise on with your passion.

Passion, when displayed in the right way, will bring emotion into the equation. Emotion can be extremely powerful. It's possible sometimes to make sales pretty much from passion alone, but more logical and analytical people will need to hear all three parts of the process in order to be fully convinced.

The best thing about passion is that if you use it well, it can mobilise people to believe in you and 'follow you'. As the entre-preneur who is doing the founder selling, you can deploy your passion to create an impact and help you start to build a tribe of followers. To do this successfully, you need to persuade innovators and early adopters to believe in you and start buying your product as soon as possible. These early clients of yours will provide important sales revenue, which will allow you to expand without having to depend on external investors.

Here are a couple of very simple examples of passion demonstrated well:

> 'Apple is not about making boxes for people to
> get their jobs done, although we do that well.
> Apple is about something more. Its core value
> is that we believe that people with passion can
> change the world for the better.'

This quote from Steve Jobs would leave any potential customer in no doubt as to how passionate these guys are.

You may not be the next Steve Jobs, and your soundbites do not have to be as dreamy as the above, but if you can come across with passion, you will persuade your prospects to believe in you. An example of the type of intelligent soundbite you might use, which is less 'salesy' but still has passion, is:

> 'We created our product because we're
> passionate about making a real difference
> to organisations in your industry, and having
> heard some of your challenges today I genu-
> inely believe that we can help you perform
> more effectively.'

Start your scale-up with passion and founder selling

So that's it: that's all you need to do to start taking control and scaling up your enterprise, using your passion when founder selling. If it sounds simple, that's because it is.

Procrastination and fear often prevent founders from kick-starting the sales growth themselves. It's important to realise that you don't have to become the perfect sales person to start making high-quality sales. By demonstrating your curiosity, delivering a compelling proposition, and using your passion to inspire your prospects, you will perform brilliantly in sales conversations.

From a buyer's perspective, you will come across as authentic, highly credible, passionate – and someone that they will be keen to do business with. What's more, your passion will help to drive you forward and to bounce back from setbacks, even when times get tough.

Once you've mastered this stage and the first sales are in the bag, your scale-up has started, but be aware that you still have a long way to go to gain real momentum.

Summary

» Use passion and founder selling to step
  up and kick-start your sales growth.

» Apply the three-step founder selling
  process:

  » Curiosity

  » Proposition

  » Passion

» To demonstrate your passion, compile
  a short list of credible, authentic,
  passionate soundbites to inspire your
  prospects.

» Don't make excuses, and forget about
  your fears: be brave, get out there, and
  personally make those all-important
  first sales.

Chapter 3

Sales Reality Check

"

*'Nothing happens until
somebody sells something.'*

ARTHUR 'RED' MOTELY

I've now explained how to use a strong proposition and your deep-rooted passion to get the first sales flowing through by your own sales efforts. But before we delve into the detail of improving your sales capability for scale-up, let's take a step back and look first at some of the common myths about selling, to make sure we are on the same page when it comes to what good selling looks like.

Let's be honest, for many people 'on the receiving end' as potential buyers, sales does not have a good name and they see conversations with sales people as best avoided wherever possible. This perception has developed for various reasons, including the fact that as consumers every one of us receives regular nuisance sales calls from overeager vendors, with financial services and telecommunications being among the worst offenders.

We also all have experience of being sold to in a retail environment, where we are approached by shop sales staff in an intrusive and unhelpful way. In addition, we regularly watch high-profile reality television shows that portray selling in a bad light. *The Apprentice* is a prime example, where the art of selling is often portrayed as being able to pitch to people in the street and negotiate in 'wheeler-dealer' style. It's no surprise, then, that many people view selling as a low-grade occupation and feel that most sales people should not be trusted. It's a real pity, but that's the reality.

Before we move on, I'm keen to emphasise that this book does not view these activities as professional selling. Professional selling is an extremely skilled and highly-regarded profession, and one that I am proud to count myself part of. We will be focusing on how to sell products professionally from one business to another – or, to put it another way, how to engage with prospects and professional buyers to provide them with solutions that can address their challenges and add value to their organisations.

It's incredibly important to me that you fully believe in the power of selling, as I know from experience the opportunities it will create for your business. But there are still a lot of legacy myths out there that might affect your perception of selling, so let's take a look at some of the most common ones, in order to clarify the reality.

Debunking the myths

Myth 1: It's just a numbers game

A lot of people think that sales is just about racking up the numbers, i.e. making lots of calls, sending out loads of emails and attending many meetings. In the context of sales it will always be true that you have to work hard and deal with a certain volume of numbers in order to grow sales revenue. But this myth can be dangerous, as doing the numbers on their own is unlikely to be enough to create the growth that your business needs.

For me, good business-to-business selling is as much about quality as quantity. You have to get the quality of your approach right first, before you start doing the numbers.

To achieve this quality, you need to:

- » create a high-quality proposition (as detailed in Chapter 1)
- » work out who is and who is not a prospect, which will save you time and improve results
- » target the right prospects and only sell to them
- » calculate your conversion rates so you can measure and improve the efficiency of your selling

Myth 2: Selling is manipulation

Unfortunately, as we've established, we've all been on the wrong end of manipulative salespeople over the years, which may have tainted our view of selling. Being salesy, sneaky or pushy, or convincing people to do something that has a win – lose outcome, is manipulative, as some of the mis-selling practices of the large banks and insurance companies have demonstrated all too clearly. If you're aiming to scale up rapidly there is no room for manipulative behaviour from you or your sales team, because it will always backfire.

If you have a good product, a strong proposition and are focusing on the right prospects, making a sale is as much in their interests as it is in yours. You will be fulfilling a need, solving a pain point, or partnering with your client to address one of their biggest challenges. That is certainly not manipulative!

Get these things right and selling is serving, which creates a virtuous circle: you are serving your clients, which in turn serves their clients; you are serving your business, which in turn serves your people; and you are serving yourself, which in turn serves your family and your community.

Myth 3: Closing sales requires high-pressure techniques

I've met many business people and CEOs who say 'I'm just not a closer.' This is to misunderstand selling, as their belief is that they have to put a lot of pressure on prospects and be a ruth-less negotiator in order to close sales. Executive sales coach Patricia Fripp of fripp.com has a refreshing take on closing:

> *'You don't close a sale, you open a relationship if you want to build a long-term, successful enterprise.'*

Experience has shown me that closing is more the result of a good product and proposition, the right prospect, and a good process. There is no special technique to closing.

You do often need to create a sense of urgency with your poten-tial client to get them to take action and commit to the order, but this is the conclusion of a professional sales process. Pros-pects will always procrastinate and a gentle nudge at the right time is wholly ethical and professional. In fact, the prospect will expect this from you and respect that you have 'asked for the business'. The stronger the relationship you have built, the more this conversation becomes natural and does not feel like high-pressure tactics from either side.

Myth 4: You need to be thick-skinned and insensitive to succeed

A good way to reframe this old-school myth is to use the term 'resilience'. Diane Coutu provides a definition of the word in an article for the *Harvard Business Review*:

> *'Resilient people possess three characteristics*
> *– a staunch acceptance of reality; a deep belief,*
> *often buttressed by strongly held values, that life*
> *is meaningful; and an uncanny ability to impro-*
> *vise. You can bounce back from hardship with*
> *just one or two of these qualities, but you will*
> *only be truly resilient with all three.'* [1]

When you get rejected, you're not normally being rejected as a person. It will most likely be something to do with your product, proposition or a weak link in your sales process, and all of these things can be improved. Be resilient and turn rejection into feedback and a learning opportunity.

Resilience is a key business skill to be learned and developed; without it you will undoubtedly take rejection personally and lose confidence over time. If you are to be successful as an entrepreneur, confidence, unshakeable self-belief, and the ability to bounce back time after time are critical traits.

---

1   Diane Coutu, 'How Resilience Works', *Harvard Business Review, May 2002* (hbr.org).

Myth 5: Selling involves cold calling and being a nuisance

With the digital revolution, the world of selling has changed dramatically. In fact, it's come a long, long way since the gritty, depressing world of door-to-door selling represented by Willy Loman in *Death of a Salesman*.[2]

When you're selling professionally to other businesses, you now thankfully don't need to go through the phone book or door-to-door, so being good at the dreaded cold calling is not necessarily important, which is good news for most of us!

Your options for contacts in this day and age are nothing like as random:

» Connecting with customers has never been easier: you can use social networking, face-to-face networking, smart email marketing and analytics – in fact a whole myriad of digital tools.

» When you 'call' someone, it can be on the back of an excellent digital icebreaker to break down the barriers and set up an open and honest conversation. When this is done right, it should not feel like a cold call.

» Your sales and marketing focus can create a 'pull' dynamic rather than the old-fashioned 'push' approach. This will generate high-quality leads to fill your pipeline, something we'll examine in detail in Chapter 4.

Myth 6: Sales people need to be extroverts or good talkers

This may surprise you, but rarely are extroverts with the 'gift of the gab' the top performers in professional selling. In fact,

---

2 Arthur Miller, *Death of a Salesman*, Methuen Drama 2010

introverts have many behavioural advantages. They use curiosity, reflection and effective listening to win sales effortlessly, without feeling the need to dominate the conversation as extroverts often do.

The Introvert Advantage[3] is a fascinating book that sheds more light on this subject; it maintains that most of us are located somewhere on a scale between extrovert and introvert (people balanced between both attributes are sometimes called 'ambiverts').[4] I've always regarded myself as being more towards the introvert end of the scale, and having initially seen it as a major barrier to being successful, I now see it as an advantage. *Quiet*[5] by Susan Cain is also a brilliant read for us all on this fascinating subject. It's worth thinking about these related points:

» Questioning, listening and thinking before you speak are key selling skills and are more important than the ability to 'talk the hind legs off a donkey'.

» 'People like people like them', which means that to get the best performance you may have to tweak your behaviour to gain the trust of different types of clients.

» Of course, extroverts are valuable too (especially as energy givers within a sales team), though they often need to learn to channel their enthusiasm, ask more questions, and listen.

3   Marti Olsen Laney, *The Introvert Advantage: How quiet people can thrive in an extrovert world*, Workman Publishing Company 2002
4   Adam Grant, The Wharton School, University of Pennsylvania.
5   Susan Cain, *Quiet: The power of introverts in a world that can't stop talking*, Penguin 2013

Myth 7: Businesses can generate orders through marketing alone, so there's no need for selling

It could be argued that in our ever-expanding online world some commodities, low-cost items, and certain other products are bought rather than sold. This may be true for some consumer products or low-value purchases for businesses, but for any business to scale up in any market segment, someone will have had to pitch and sell ideas to partners, retailers, etc. Even in these examples, face-to-face selling is still happening. For any business with high-value products or substantial order values, you will undoubtedly need to master the art of face-to-face selling to grow rapidly.

Sales teams are smaller than they were a decade ago as the customer can now find a lot more information online before any selling takes place. So the role of the sales person has changed, becoming more consultative, advisory and adding value. David Maister expertly explained this mode of communicating and selling effectively as far back as 2001, in *The Trusted Advisor*.[6]

For you as a scale-up entrepreneur, this change is a great opportunity, as building your sales team is now more about quality than quantity. In the early days, you should focus on building a high-quality, specialised sales team comprising you yourself and one or two other talented, driven, credible sales people who are seen by the clients as trusted advisors. We will look further at how to build your perfect team in Chapter 5.

---

6   David Maister, Charles Green, and Robert Galford, *The Trusted Advisor*, Simon & Schuster 2002

Myth 8: Professional recruitment and training always result in high-performing sales people

Taking on a proven sales person is no guarantee of sales success. Equally, putting a sales person through a proven sales training course does not mean they will perform well. In sales there are few guarantees, which is what makes it interesting and challenging! It can be a bit like Real Madrid paying a huge sum of money to recruit a star striker and then ensuring the player has all the right coaching, training and development. They should perform well and score lots of goals, but it doesn't always happen!

Recruitment and development will be important for your business, but do it in a considered, cost-effective way that works for your entrepreneurial culture. It's also critical to get the people blend right, as if people feel they are an integral part of a close-knit team they will perform better.

Modern selling: your opportunity

So, this reality check may have produced some genuine surprises for you. But more importantly, I hope it's given you more of a real feel for what modern, professional selling is, and what it is not.

Debunking these myths shows that anyone can become good at sales and that there are absolutely no barriers for you as an entrepreneur to start with founder selling and then create a powerful sales engine to scale up your business.

You have a great opportunity, both to become good at sales yourself and to build a great sales team in your own image. With a strong sales focus, you can now take control of your own entrepreneurial scale-up.

Summary

» There are many myths about selling – forget about them and reframe selling in your mind as a positive driver of growth.

» Focus on selling your products professionally, to provide your clients with solutions that can address challenges and add value.

» Believe in a sales philosophy that will give you the focus, control, autonomy, and confidence to drive the scale-up of your business.

Chapter 4

Pipeline

*'Keep your sales pipeline full by
prospecting continuously. Always
have more people to see than
you have time to see them.'*

BRIAN TRACY

Every company in the world that sells successfully to other businesses has a sales 'pipeline'. A pipeline is exactly as described – a pipe into which you put leads at one end, which hopefully will become good prospects, and eventually pop out the other end of the pipe as customers. As you've now started to make some sales, it's the right time to create your own pipeline, to organise and manage the process of converting leads into customers.

Surprisingly, many companies are not adept at filling and managing their pipelines, and I think one of the reasons for this is that they overcomplicate the process. As the leader of an entrepreneurial business that needs sales (and lots of them) popping out of your pipeline, you need a simple process to establish and maintain your pipeline.

First you need to pinpoint exactly who your target customers are. You then need to start filling your pipeline by generating leads. In order to make high-value sales, you then need to have sales meetings with these prospects (we will look at performance in these sales meetings in Chapters 6–8), and finally you need to ensure efficient, professional follow-up to close sales.

Creating your pipeline

Before you start putting leads into your pipeline, your first move is to invest in a Customer Relationship Management (CRM) system to help you to organise and manage your pipeline process. There are dozens of available cloud based options, but take your time and choose carefully as this system will become a critical business tool. Bear in mind that you need a CRM which is good for both sales and marketing and cost effective for a small business. The right, easy-to-use CRM will automate your entire pipeline process and ensure that you not only manage it efficiently but that you can also monitor your sales effectiveness at an organisational and individual level and identify key trends and areas for improvement.

Running an effective sales pipeline is very simple – you need to use your sales and marketing activities to move a prospect along a pipeline from one end to the other (from a lead to a sale). We will look further at how you should do this as the chapter moves on. When a sale is closed, it pops out of the other end of the pipeline as a new customer, to be looked after by your Project Management/Account Management team.

When you first start creating a pipeline, it can be beneficial to bring it to life by also viewing a practical model. There is a simple, visual pipeline outlined in the pragmatic book *The Gorillas*

Want Bananas[1] in the chapter "Fill the Pipeline". It illustra
a model that you can actually print out and stick on your wall
and chart how you move prospects along the pipeline (using
Post-Its) from left to right until they become sales/customers.
It also gets you to start thinking about specific tactics you can
use to move people from "Suspects" (Complete Strangers)
right through to "Customers" (Evangelists). Well worth a look
when you start your pipeline building activities.

In the rest of this chapter we will focus on making sure you
generate the right leads and also examine some practical
techniques to move them along your pipeline.

Who are your target customers?

Now that you have a CRM to organise and manage your pipeline, before you start filling it, identifying your target customers
is the first step. In your headlong pursuit of growth, there is
a big risk that you will burn time and money chasing sales
to any company in any sector that will buy your product. Be
careful – I wouldn't recommend this!

I have form for this. At BigHand, we sold (as a value added
reseller) our first product to anyone who would take it. For the
first four years, we travelled around the UK a lot and made
lots of sales to big-name clients in every sector imaginable.
You may be thinking, 'What's the problem here? This sounds
great!' And it did seem to be great for a while, but we eventually
realised it was high energy and high cost.

Our scattergun selling approach meant that generating new
leads was hard work, as we were not getting word of mouth
recommendations. Ultimately, we had to accept the reality that

---

1   Debbie Jenkins & Joe Gregory, *The Gorillas Want Bananas,* Lean Marketing Press 2003

this approach would not result in enough high-value sales to enable us to scale up rapidly in the way that we wanted.

After much frustration and brainstorming, a thought popped into my head. During my postgraduate marketing degree course at the University of Strathclyde, one of the lecturers had quoted a well-known business phrase: 'Get big, get niche or get out!'

The penny dropped... we were too small to 'get big', we were still ambitious and didn't want to 'get out', so we needed to 'get niche'.

Niche focus

When we found and focused on our niche market – the legal market – things really started to happen for us. We developed our own product and sold this one product into this one market sector. It sounds very simple, but this is when our world changed and we began to scale up at speed.

My business partner Steve had been concerned about whether one niche market was big enough for us to be successful, but as we started to penetrate the legal market we realised there were several advantages to concentrating on one market:

» 'Niching' allows you to gain a deep understanding of those in your chosen market – their pains, their aspirations and what makes them tick.

» Focusing on the right niche leads to more business, not less, and can be very profitable.

» Word of mouth within a niche spreads your reputation quickly without much marketing spend, leading to recommendations and referrals.

» Relevant flagship reference sites and testimonials help to convert prospects into clients, speeding up your lead to sale conversion rate.

How to find your niche and your perfect market

Identifying your niche market may come easily to you, but if it doesn't seem obvious you need to do your research and think long and hard. The temptation is to say, 'OK, at the moment we are trying to sell to the world, so let's cut that down to three or four sectors.' That makes sense in theory, but with your limited resources you may dilute your focus.

Your ideal niche could be a market to which you are currently selling and in which you seem to be making a real difference for your clients. Or it could be a vertical sector, such as the property sector, that you have always admired as a high potential market.

Before you settle on your perfect niche, you may need to do some test selling for a few weeks or months to see if your research and gut feel are right. It's also obviously sensible to have a transition period during which you keep selling into other sectors to keep revenues up. Also, bear in mind that you can tweak your niche as your business develops. As we progressed through the UK legal market, we realised that to maintain our sales growth rate we should start selling internationally, and we thought Europe was the obvious place to start.

But Europe is a big continent and we heeded the words of a former colleague (from Dragon Systems, now Nuance) who had recommended we 'focus primarily on the beer-drinking countries, not the wine-drinking countries.' What he meant was that we should focus on northern Europe, as culturally Dragon had found these countries were easier to sell to. So the Netherlands, Belgium and Scandinavia formed our revised

European niche and that advice proved to be sound as we quickly penetrated Europe.

Focus on building your pipeline

Once you have found the right target market, you need to commit to it and focus on it fully to build your pipeline. I've found four simple steps work well for starting to fill up your pipeline. You may have to juggle these steps to keep the momentum up:

1. Flagship reference sales to kick-start your pipeline

Ok, so it's time to start filling your pipeline with good quality leads and prospects. The starting point is specifically to target some key firms and decision-makers within your chosen niche that you want to be your first sales and reference sites.

This is not just a question of finding a list of the top companies in the sector and targeting the top few. You have to use far more precision than this:

» Do your research to find early adopters, as they will be good firms to target.

» Network like crazy – join relevant LinkedIn groups, attend events, conferences and awards dinners in your target market to build relationships with key influencers.

» Build a list of the top 20 senior decision-makers and thought leaders in your chosen sector, and connect up with them (the firms must be of high quality, with a strong reputation).

 » Ask your top 20 individually for advice as to how to sell your product into their sector (at this stage it's critical that you do not try to sell your product to them).

» Build strong relationships via ongoing conversations/coffees/lunches/dinners.

» When the time is right (only you can judge when this is) meet them individually to discuss your proposition and the possibility of them becoming one of your first flagship reference sites.

» Entice them with extremely favourable 'pioneer pricing'; in return they should provide introductions to other firms, reference calls, and site visits for interested prospects, and agree to be profiled via social media/ PR coverage.

» Gradually rack up these reference site sales and once you get to five to ten sites you will gain some serious momentum and notice that your pipeline starts filling quicker as your name starts to get known and others in the sector sit up and take notice.

This flagship reference model worked brilliantly for us when top 20 UK law firm Ashurst agreed to roll out our BigHand digital dictation software and become our first flagship law firm reference site with over 1000 users (this was also the first global legal enterprise digital dictation project).

We had worked extremely hard to build a relationship and reputation with Ashurst, and when the CIO, Chris White, signed off our biggest ever order, he told us he trusted us implicitly and, interestingly, that he never felt at any stage that he was 'being sold to'.

After the roll-out, Chris agreed to host a flagship event at Ashurst's smart offices in central London, and the resulting successful evening, together with a PR and marketing blitz, was the launch pad for BigHand to start its rapid scale-up in the legal market.

2. Create your marketing engine

In order to fill your sales pipeline, you need to ensure that you have a strong marketing engine. The starting point is a solid, distinctive proposition (Chapter 1).

Your first priority should be to recruit a talented marketing executive. Believe me, life will become much easier for you when you take on a talented, driven individual, ideally fresh from a specialised digital marketing course at university. This is a key hire, as this person, working closely with you, will be able to co-ordinate the lead generation necessary to fill your pipeline through the following key activities:

» Using your CRM as the hub of your pipeline building and management activities. (Make sure your marketing executive has the skill set and the digital sharpness to run this CRM expertly, as a CRM is only as good as the way it is run).

» Your **website** must be super-professional, crisp, classy and easy to navigate (it must be better than those of your main competitors!) and it should always include:

  » super content: high value and relevant to your niche, with slick capture forms, calls to action and downloadable content (make sure you capture visitor data via analytics);

  » short videos/animated movies are always crowd-pleasers. There are several packages available (Videoscribe is superb)[2] that enable you easily

---

2 Videoscribe from Sparkol, sparkol.com.

to create cost-effective, high impact videos yourselves;

» online health checks useful for your target market
(e.g., for CIOs to analyse the performance of their
IT team); and

» advanced analytics packages to provide you with
named leads from among your website visitors, for
swift sales follow-up.

» All organisations must have a decent presence on **social
media**. Make sure your marketing executive focuses
on social media activities that can contribute to lead
generation and monitors success rates closely.

» Classy **e-shots** can generate some good leads, as long
as they have strong calls to action, such as invitations
to exclusive events you create and run yourselves.

3. Fill your diary with high quality sales meetings

Your marketing executive will become a key member of your
team, but you can't rely on this person to build your pipeline
on their own. It's important that you personally step up on a
weekly basis and get stuck into generating leads and booking
sales meetings for yourself.

Some practical tips that I have found work well include:

» setting aside Monday and Tuesday every week to focus
on booking appointments (a great way to fill your diary);

» booking sales meetings in for Wednesday to Friday,
aiming to fill your diary by booking at least three meetings for each sales meeting day;

» asking for referrals from people you get to know well, or who you have sold to. Referral introductions – especially when you ask personally – will quickly lead to high quality meetings which will increase your chances of closing quickly (Dale Carnegie once said '91% of customers would give referrals, but only 11% of sales people ask for referrals',[3] so get asking!);

» using LinkedIn regularly – spend a lot of time on this network, connecting with and messaging your target market, posting thought-provoking ideas and linking to your personal blog (the advanced features available in LinkedIn Premium products can be useful for compiling your 'dream' list of people/firms and starting to connect with them);

» harnessing the power of email: it's also important to make sure when you are emailing prospects daily that your brand stands out. Most email signatures get stripped by firewalls and look scrappy and unimpressive. Invest in a specialist email branding product (such as Rocketseed),[4] to keep your brand looking sharp and to turn all your day-to-day emails into an opportunity to generate leads.

4. Become a Key Person of Influence

A smart guy I chaired on an entrepreneurial panel last year, Daniel Priestley, has written a great book for entrepreneurs, *Key Person of Influence*, in which he says:

> 'Across all industries, the top opportunities go directly to a small group who present themselves as "Key People of Influence" in that field.'[5]

---

3   Dale Carnegie, *How to Win Friends and Influence People*, Random House Group 2006.
4   Rocketseed, rocketseed.com
5   Daniel Priestley, *Key Person of Influence*, Rethink Press 2014.

This is exactly what you, as the entrepreneur with the vision and the passion, want to become. I'd encourage you to read Daniel's book (or attend his KPI programme) to understand fully how to achieve this.

For now, using a selection of the following quick ideas can position you in this way.

> » Publish – one of Daniel's ideas is that you should constantly publish your thoughts and opinions on blogs, LinkedIn, etc, to profile yourself as a thought leader in your space.

> » Put yourself forward for speaking slots at all the key events in your niche and do short, sharp, memorable, non-promotional talks to get everyone talking about you.

> » Network like crazy, at every event going. (I know a great guy, Christopher Barrat, who can teach you how to network face-to-face, as it's important you become great at this.)[6]

> » Create a super-cool, themed series of drinks events (e.g., 'Thursday Tech Top-ups'), which create a buzz within your target market and give you a chance to showcase yourself and warm up people in your pipeline.

Your pipeline at the core of your sales focus

Once you are focused on one niche, this whole process becomes much easier, but maintaining your pipeline must become part of this focus. Don't forget that you also need to disqualify prospects and clean out your pipeline regularly. If you've not managed to move a lead along the pipeline after

---

6   Christopher Barrat, Greystone Consulting, http://mc.greystone.co.uk.

a few weeks of trying, it's probably worth moving it out of the sales pipeline and putting it on a marketing list to receive regular company updates.

It's not easy to fill and manage a quality pipeline, but to do it well you need to make an impact. To achieve this, you should innovate continually, dream up exciting ideas, be brave, and make people think, 'Wow, I just keep hearing about this company and they are really impressing me. I must look into them further...'

If you can create that sort of impact, you will start to gain serious momentum.

And here's the thing: the more sales you make, the more momentum you will gain, increasing the pace at which your pipeline fills with quality leads and increasing the pace at which you make sales.

As you continue to build and refine your pipeline, there will come a time when you (and your fellow directors) will have too many leads to follow up yourselves – yes, it will happen if you get this bit right! When this happens, it's time to start building your dream sales team and this is what we will explore next.

Summary

» Your pipeline is at the heart of your sales and marketing activities for achieving successful scale-up.

» Invest in a flexible CRM system to organise, automate and report back on the success of your sales pipeline management process.

» Decide who your target customers are: focusing on a niche market enables your reputation to spread quickly and results in faster sales growth.

» Follow the four-step process for successful pipeline management:

  » develop flagship reference clients;

  » create a strong, cost effective, marketing engine (organised by your marketing executive via an excellent CRM);

  » focus on filling your diary with high-quality sales meetings; and

  » position yourself as a Key Person of Influence (KPI).

» Always maintain your pipeline as the core of your sales focus, to continually improve your lead-to-sale timescales and conversion rates.

Chapter 5
People

'There is no such thing as great talent without great will power.'

BALZAC

This chapter helps you to move from selling personally to building a sales team to share the load with you. By now, you have a strong product and a compelling proposition. You have proved that as the founder with the passion you can make sales and you have started to build your pipeline. You now understand the critical importance of selling to your chances of scale-up success. But understandably, you are ambitious and impatient to make more sales and grow faster.

We all know that people are the most important part of our lives – our family, our friends, our colleagues. As human beings, we naturally want to spend time with people we love, like, trust and respect, and you must remember this when you start to build your own sales team, as this team will become your extended family. You will want to work with people whose company you enjoy (you will probably spend as much time with them as with your own family), people who share your vision and values, and people that you trust implicitly to get the job done.

However, you're only ready to move into this people phase of your development once you have built some good flagship reference sites and have money in the bank to invest in building your sales engine. Ideally, you'll continue to be a player manager for some time still, as it's important you lead from the front and gain respect from your growing team by getting your sleeves rolled up and making sales yourself. By doing this, you will also be able to relate to your sales people by understanding the objections and challenges awaiting them in the market and being able to help your people handle them confidently.

This is a critical and very exciting phase, and you'll start to feel real momentum for the first time as your business surges forward with the collective efforts of a driven, motivated sales team behind it!

What will your sales culture look like?

Before you start recruiting, you must first work out what kind of sales team culture you are going to create. By clearly defining this, you'll find it easier to attract and inspire the right talent to join you. If your new recruits are clear about your culture and about what is expected of them, you're much more likely to meet their expectations and retain core people throughout your scale-up journey.

It's your business and your sales team, so it's crucial that you believe in your sales culture. Your sales culture and your sales people should be very much in your own image.

Six key pillars of a high-performance culture

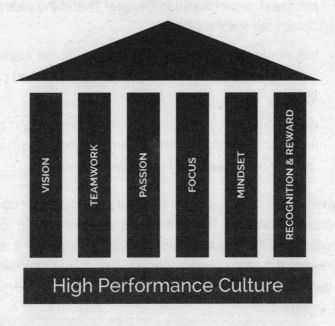

I was always extremely proud of the sales culture that we built in our tech firm. We created a high-performance culture in which people always strove to do their best, worked as a team to hit their targets, and gritted their teeth to bounce back from disappointments in a determined, optimistic way.

Some of it happened by design and some by trial and error, but rather than doing all the hard yards yourself, make use of the list of six key pillars described below to help you to start shaping your very own high-performance culture. Obviously, you can continually evolve your culture in the way that suits your growing business:

Vision: It's essential to communicate a clear vision of what you are trying to achieve as a team:

» make sure people understand that this is the 'why' of teamwork (as explored in Chapter 1) and the glue that holds your team together;

» talk about and write down your vision as an inspiring sales team mission that your people can live and work by; and

» print it out in an eye-catching, glossy banner and post it up on the sales team wall as a motivational reminder! (as well as virtually on your CRM/intranet 'walls'.)

Teamwork: People in a sales team are often a collection of individuals who work for themselves and not for the team. By contrast, in the very best sports teams, everyone is a team player and the team always comes first. If you can create this team culture, you will work well together and outperform your competition:

» inspirational and fun team events are a great way for your team to bond, so invest in and organise a variety of catch-ups regularly to surprise, delight and keep your team fresh. (I once got my guys into the office for the start of a quarterly strategic sales team meeting and then revealed we were all going to a Cotswolds boutique hotel for two days of 'inspiration' – inspiring video workshop sessions, quad biking, pub lunches, great dinners and team bonding. By exceeding expectations, motivation and sales performance were sky high in the weeks that followed!)

» Sir Ian McGeechan once told me that one of the success secrets of the British & Irish Lions rugby team culture is to bond as quickly as possible on tour with super-simple techniques such as 'rooming' together and regular coffee catch-ups after training.

Passion: Build passion by celebrating effort as well as success, staying positive and making it fun!

» don't assume your people will be as passionate as you are; you need to help them develop their passion for your business.

» think about ways you can make your people fall in love with your business so that clients will fall in love with them.

Focus: If you can train your people to master the art of focus, they will perform well. My experience is that most companies assume their people are focused, which may or may not be true. But in the modern digital world there can be so many distractions pinging in and out of devices that you need to think about:

» getting together with your sales people regularly in the sales office to work together as a team;

» knowing how and when to put the blinkers on them so they focus 100% on selling; and

» leading them in keeping 'selling time' sacrosanct: your people shouldn't be writing proposals or doing research during these focused selling periods; during selling time you should be selling – on the phone, social selling, booking meetings and sales meeting follow up – nothing else!

Mindset: For your team to perform well, every person needs to have a focused, positive mindset, so make this one of your core team mantras:

» in a small, positive entrepreneurial business you don't have room for negative, defensive, energy-sappers (you need 'radiators' rather than 'drains')

» we were privileged to have England rugby star Will Greenwood MBE speak at The Sales Club, and he mentioned that the England Rugby World Cup winning team had a mindset that was 'half rock, half sponge', i.e., people have to be tough, but they should also soak up all the new ideas and coaching tips to keep improving. Committing to a simple and memorable team mindset like this is a great idea.

Recognition and reward: Creating an aspirational, top-notch recognition and reward structure can be a huge motivator for your team members. A programme that would be the envy of the world's top companies can allow you to punch above your weight:

» structure your bonus/commission system for individuals and the team.

» if you put 'overachievement accelerators' in target and bonus-based schemes, people will keep driving hard to hit targets and go beyond (with commission based schemes, if someone makes a few sales in a particular quarter they can start feeling comfortable and ease off, as they know they're going to get paid for any sales they have already made).

» team targets will help to foster team spirit and meeting them can be recognised with non-monetary, aspirational rewards: trips away, latest gizmos as gifts, etc. (The *Harvard Business Review* recently featured a company that created an internal, online team fantasy football league, with the winners being the team who achieved the best metrics across various sales categories. It proved to be hugely motivational and improved performance massively.)[1]

1   Ethan Bernstein and Hayley Blunden: *The Sales Director Who Turned Work into a Fantasy Sports Competition*, *Harvard Business Review*, March 2015 (hbr.org).

» recognition is a huge motivator: it is a psychological fact that people long for acceptance and recognition. Striving for and receiving an award fills people with pride and a sense of achievement, so create some superb awards initiatives, perhaps starting with a simple 'sales person of the month' award.

» continue to innovate as your sales team grows and don't be afraid to be brave and bold with your recognition and reward programme as it has to remain current and fresh to keep inspiring your people.

Ten Top Tips for hiring your perfect team

Now that you have defined and started to flesh out what your sales culture will look like, it's time to start hiring! Recruitment is never easy, but if you are to succeed, you need to do this well. Everyone has a different view on the best way to recruit and there will always be some luck involved.

I'm not a professional recruiter, but here is a set of ten simple rules that have worked for me:

1. Recruit people who live close enough to the office to be in there regularly, as this will massively help your bonding and team performance; regional and virtual working can come later, after an office-based team is firing on all cylinders.

2. Lead hiring yourself to ensure quality control and because you, as the founder, will attract the best people, but get admin support to help sift through CVs and put the best ones in front of you.

3. Create a precise job specification itemising exactly who you are looking for and what you expect them to do.

(In the early days, I prefer to focus on relatively recent graduates as they'll be affordable, driven and keen to learn.)

4. Use your primary social networks to post your job opportunities and also consider a reputable online recruitment company with a fixed fee for a job advertisement (for example, milkround.com for graduates).

5. Personally conduct a day of telephone interviews on the best CVs (approximately 30 minutes per interview).

6. Shortlist the top handful of candidates and invite them in for one-hour face-to-face interviews.

   » Spend time building a rapport with them, as they have to like you as well as you liking them.

   » Look closely for the key traits of curiosity and passion, to see if they possess these or if you feel that with coaching they could develop them.

7. Always do second interviews, even if you feel certain that someone is right, as people often come across differently at second interview.

   » At the second interview include a practical sales exercise requiring selling skills, to see how they perform under pressure. (By way of example, you could explain what curiosity is and ask them to question you as if you were a prospect).

   » Ideally, bring in one of your current sales people so you can get their opinion on the shortlisted candidates (and check chemistry).

8. Never make a job offer on the spot, always sleep on it!

9. Before you make a job offer, ask yourself three final 'reality check' questions about the candidate:

 » Will this person work hard and be prepared to go the extra mile?

 » Will you be able to coach this person, as it's critical that they are not defensive and that they buy into the philosophy of continual improvement?

 » Will they fit into your sales culture?

10. If the answers are all 'Yes', you are in business (assuming they are as excited as you) and you can start making job offers. (It can be a good idea to adopt a 'Noah's Ark' approach and sign up two sales people from the same recruitment round who you think will get on well, so they have a buddy to start with and you can train them together.)

The above are only guidelines and obviously you should also use your own common sense and gut feel to hire the right team for your business.

Give your new recruit(s) time to bed in and start making sales. Don't go chasing more bodies until your current team is performing, as the quality of your people is much more important than the quantity.

Leadership – what kind of leader are you going to be?

It's always an exciting time when you start to hire and build your team. But the excitement will only last if your team perform to expectations. And for that to happen, you will need to become a leader who motivates and inspires them. The bottom line is that they need to respect you. So, what kind of leader are you going to be? Have you thought about this? If you haven't, now is the time.

As I explained earlier in this chapter, you must feel completely comfortable with your leadership style and your leadership style must complement your sales culture. Do not try to be something that you are not, as this won't work and will stress you out as you will be acting out a role.

I believe that strong leadership does not necessarily come from being the most charismatic person in the world; it comes from building trust and respect with your people. To achieve that, demonstrating the following behaviours can be very effective for all of those who lead teams:

1. Leading by example: if you are prepared to be a player manager by stepping up and selling, as well as leading, you will build enduring credibility, loyalty and respect.

2. Coaching: it's critical to establish a coaching culture early on, as if your people are to improve, you will have to coach them continually and they have to feel they want to co-coach and support each other. All feedback should be taken in the right spirit, in a quest for continual improvement. (World-renowned athletics coach Charles Van Commenee told me at one of our events that all good leaders should spend a lot of what he called 'tracksuit time' building trust with their people and that the best way to do this is to 'always ask questions and listen.')

3. Being firm but fair: this has always been one of my key personal leadership philosophies, and it's clear that many of the top leaders in sport and business are firm individuals. Treating your people with firmness and consistency will gain you their long-term respect.

4. Praising effort over results: this may sound like an unusual tip, but psychologically it is important for your team's motivation. (We had Matthew Syed, ex-table tennis player and sportswriter for *The Times*, as a keynote speaker at The Sales Club, and one of the core findings from his best-selling book *Bounce* was that it is much more motivational to 'praise your people for effort, than to praise them for results.')[2]

Building the performance of your people

If you are leading your people well, they shouldn't just be seeing their role as a 'job'. They should feel motivated, energised and excited about the potential to develop and have a great career working with you and your company.

You will know they feel this way as you will witness first-hand their drive and energy in the way they operate, and your close relationship means they will be honest with you if they are feeling at all demotivated. They will tell their partners, family and friends what a great business they work for and how much they enjoy being part of a fantastic sales team. They will be proud to work for you and you will be proud to lead them.

But being a leader can be a lonely, high-pressure job, and it's worth noting that it is unlikely your team will give you praise for being a superb leader (much as children don't ever say, 'Mummy and Daddy, I just wanted to say you're both doing a brilliant job looking after us, so thanks very much!').

So it's critical that you, as the leader, retain your self-belief, remain resilient and trust you are on the right course, while having a flexible 'growth mindset' to allow you to continue

---

2   Matthew Syed, *Bounce: The myth of talent and the power of practice*, Harper Collins 2011.

evolving and improving. Ultimately, you need to take your sense of satisfaction and pride from the way your people develop, the way they perform, the results they produce, and the loyalty they show. If these indicators are all good, you will start gaining some serious sales momentum.

Also, don't forget that with every day that goes by, you and your team can keep improving. If you foster this philosophy of continual improvement your people will continue to make sales and drive your business inexorably closer to genuine scale-up success.

Summary

» People are the most important part of your business, so invest huge amounts of your personal time and energy to build a great sales team you will enjoy spending time with.

» Your 'people phase' should start when:

  » you have built some good flagship client reference sites;

  » you are generating more leads for your pipeline than you can deal with yourself; and

  » you have money in the bank to start expanding.

» Define, create and build an inspiring high-performance sales culture that makes you and your people feel passionate and proud.

» Take control of recruitment personally, to ensure you build a high quality team.

» Be the kind of leader who commands respect, to secure long-term commitment from your people.

» Believe that you and your people can keep getting better every day that goes by, in a quest for continual improvement.

Chapter 6

Performance 1
Prepare for your Perfect Sales Meeting

*'Plan your work and work
your plan.'*

NAPOLEON HILL

Sales success, when you are selling your products to other businesses, hinges around sales meetings with potential buyers. Now that you have started to hire and develop talented, driven people, your focus should shift to how your team members perform in sales meetings, as this will determine whether your business makes enough sales ultimately to be successful.

Everything in the book so far has helped you to create credibility, grab attention and gain an audience with the top people. Building a strong lead generation pipeline, as explained in Chapter 4, will ensure you create opportunities to connect with your prospects in face-to-face meetings, and in Chapter 5 we examined the critical importance of hiring the right people for being able to scale up successfully.

Now you need to make sure that you and your people perform in each and every meeting, regardless of who's in the room or the level of pressure to succeed. If you get it right, this is the fun part of selling. You and your sales team have the opportunity to meet interesting people, create strong relationships, showcase your product in a 'live' situation, and use your selling skills to impress your prospects. You are not there just to have a nice chat. You obviously have to get on with the other people in the room, but there's a lot more to it than that...

This series of three performance chapters moves us into the sharp end of sales and sets out the key elements of an effective sales meeting – not least the critical planning and preparation you need to do beforehand. We'll then delve into the detail of each stage of a typical meeting, sharing practical techniques you can use to get the results you need.

Meetings with multiple decision makers

In these Performance chapters we will focus on multi-person meetings where the attendees include you (and possibly one of your colleagues) and two or more attendees from the potential client's side. In the advice that follows, I am making the following assumptions about these meetings:

» this type of meeting is the first key meeting with a prospect, and is where you will make (or set up) the majority of your high-value sales;

» these meetings will include some or all of the key decision makers and influencers for the potential client; and

> » these meetings will generally be held in a meeting room at the potential client's office.

One-to-one meetings will tend to have a less formal structure, but some of the ideas discussed here can often still be relevant. One-to-one meetings, such as 'coffee meetings', are best used to build relationships and credibility, so that your prospect agrees to move the sales conversation on to a multi-person meeting.

Now you may well be thinking, 'I'm pretty sure I'm already fairly good in sales meeting situations; it's pretty much common sense...' Well, be open-minded, because there is a fine line between success and failure in terms of performance and results. And there is a lot more to the science of performance in sales meetings than meets the eye.

What do we mean by 'performance'?

So what do we mean when we talk about improving performance?

I think the best place to look for parallels to help us in business is in our top sports teams. One of the most successful concepts is the 'aggregation of marginal gains', pioneered by legends like Sir Clive Woodward and Sir Dave Brailsford well over a decade ago. This entails continually seeking tiny percentage point improvements in everything we do, in the belief that all the marginal improvements and refinements will add up to make a tangible difference when you're aiming to improve performance and produce the best results.

The results these guys have kick-started show that this philosophy seems to work! In fact, as I write, Britain's Olympic team, at the Rio 2016 Olympics, have just produced their best-ever medal-winning performance, outstripping the phenomenal

London 2012 results by finishing second in the medals table, just above China! Interestingly, the philosophy of continual improvement through marginal gains is regularly mentioned by British coaches and competitors as the primary factor driving this success.

For me, performance in sales meetings is exactly the same. As the sales leader, you have a responsibility to be constantly looking for new ways to improve your performance in these situations. To start you off, we will provide you with a solid, structured performance model, which you can then continue to build and improve on with your team. If you get your performance in sales meetings spot on, good sales results will inevitably follow.

Why would a prospect agree to meet with you?

Performance in sales meetings is important for many reasons, not least because attending sales meetings is expensive when you take into account salaries, travel time and expenses. I've met many sales people over the years who will always try to get face to face with any customer in order to 'do the numbers'. It's an admirable attitude, but is it the right approach nowadays?

We all know that potential buyers can now find out a lot about your product online, and this stark statistic from the Corporate Executive Board shows that the digital world we live in makes it even harder to engage with buyers: '... 57% of the purchase decision is complete before a customer even calls a supplier.'[1] Whether you like it or not, buyers now see less reason to have sales meetings with vendors like you, especially early on in the purchase decision-making process.

---

1   Corporate Executive Board (best practice insight and technology company), cebglobal.com.

So what does this really mean for you? In Chapter 4 we explored how to use leads from your pipeline building activities to start booking meetings. To take this to the next level, and to make sure that people agree to meet with you and that the meetings you book are highly effective, you need to think through the answers to the following questions:

> » Why should a potential client want to meet with you? It's important to put yourself in their shoes so you can consider how to convince them to meet up.

> » What value can you provide them with at the meeting that they won't find online, which will make them keen to meet you?

> » How are you going to articulate the value of the meeting to them in a way that makes them think, 'It would definitely be worthwhile having a meeting'? (Remember that this is where a good proposition will help.)

If you can get the answers to these questions right and communicate clearly the value you will be adding, you will start to book meetings that are valuable for both you and your potential clients.

Building a top sales meeting

Just booking meetings is not enough to ensure top performance in the meeting. Once they are in your diary, your job is not done! In fact, it's just the beginning. Surprisingly, many sales people rest on their laurels once a meeting is booked and assume that the meeting itself, in a few weeks' time, will go brilliantly, with very little further contact.

However, I have found that the following process is critically important for making the best of every sales meeting opportunity.

This process uses your curiosity skills, which we explored in Chapter 2, to find out important information and uncover needs. If you ask the right questions, your potential client will not find your approach intrusive. Far from it – they will normally be flattered and impressed by your desire to get a comprehensive understanding of their business and its challenges.

Building

When you are booking meetings, the most important thing is to impress the prospect enough to get the meeting in the diary. But you will only find out so much information on this first call or email. You now need to 'build' the multi-person meeting to give yourself a clearer picture of the world in which your prospect lives and how you might help them.

You can build the meeting over the telephone, or you can suggest a meeting with your contact for coffee (if you happen to be located close to your prospect this is the ideal scenario, as it allows you to fact-find and build a relationship so there will be a bond between you at the meeting itself). Whatever the circumstances, when you get to the meeting, you should have the following information already:

> size and shape of the firm

> prospect's role within the firm

» details of the team that the prospect runs

» key challenges for your prospect

» the department that might benefit most from your product in a first-phase project (it's always useful to explore potential users in advance and invite a person from this department)

» who the decision makers for a potential project are (can these people attend as well?)

» technical information: seek an introduction to someone in the IT department to find out key information on their systems– it will put you on the front foot in the meeting and allow you to pre-empt any potential technical objections

» the budget – it's good to go in knowing what the budget process is for new investment and who holds the purse strings

Proposition teaser

Send a 'teaser' piece of high impact collateral/video to your prospect after the building phase (see the examples in the 'Create your Marketing Engine' section of Chapter 4). This will allow you to:

» spread this quality information via your contact to the other attendees, so they turn up relatively well informed (a multi-person meeting where people know nothing about you will feel like hard work!)

» give the prospect a feel for your product (and time to think about how it might help them)

» start to build interest and desire for your product, to put you on the front foot before the meeting

Confirming

Confirming the meeting a couple of days beforehand may sound an obvious piece of advice, but it's still hugely important. People's diaries can change suddenly and your meeting may be low on their priority list. The last thing you want to do is make a trip and turn up to be told that the meeting has been postponed or that only one junior person will be attending. To mitigate this risk, it is worth:

>> calling your key contact two to three days beforehand to check that everything is in order as agreed in your previous chats, and that the main people are still committed to attending

>> sending a quick email on the morning of the meeting to double-check something, for example, that they have the right audio-visual kit in the meeting room and you can get onto their guest Wi-Fi. (This is really just an excuse to get in touch with them; if there is any problem with the meeting they will let you know at this stage.)

Is it possible to over prepare?

Absolutely not! Preparation is critical in order for you to achieve your best performance in the meeting itself. If you plan and prepare in the right way it will allow you to start building a strong relationship, acquire information, and establish needs, which will help you to position your proposition in such a way as to make them feel they need your help.

There is nothing like going into a sales meeting feeling well informed, confident, and tuned into the specific benefits of your product for your prospect. When you are running a sales team, you will want to know that your planning and preparation processes mean that your people are also fully prepared for each and every meeting.

If you've followed the process above, you should now have plenty of information, an idea of the challenges/pain points of your target client, and a good idea of how you will approach the sales meeting. So all you need to do now is print out all the notes you have taken during the building and confirming stages (from your CRM), digest them in advance, and take them to the meeting along with your blank notepad.

Before we go into the meeting itself, I'm going to introduce one more key tool that should make a big difference to your live performance within the meeting.

Sales meeting model: SPQ

Your biggest challenges in any meeting will be time, and structure and control (or lack of it). If you go in without a plan, agenda or structure, you will probably lose control of the meeting and it will degenerate into wide-ranging chit-chat that will not lead anywhere.

After attending dozens of meetings like this with sales team colleagues, I became increasingly frustrated at our regular poor performance in these meetings, which resulted in numerous wasted opportunities. So, to turn things around, take back control, and give my sales team an easy-to-use tool to enable them to perform to their potential throughout the meeting, I created 'SPQ' (standing for 'sales performance quarters'), a simple visual model that I find works brilliantly!

SPQ Model

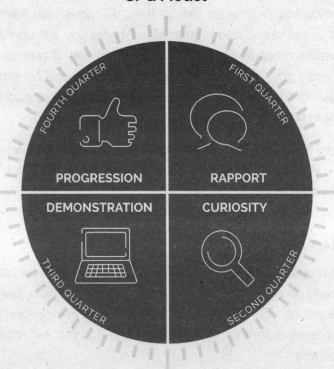

This model will help you to keep track of time, remain aware of the key areas you want to cover, and adhere to your planned structure for the meeting without relying on scripts. You'll be able to maintain your focus on impressing prospects, all the while heading towards your desired outcome and handling responses and feedback deftly.

Although the model is extremely simple to follow, I'll explain in detail how to use it in the next two chapters.

The good news is that you are now fully prepared for your sales meeting! You're feeling informed, positive and upbeat about the way you're going to manage and control this meeting. That's a great position to be in before you arrive at the meeting itself.

Summary

» 'Performance' entails giving an impressive account of your business and your product in a sales meeting, regardless of who's in the room and the level of pressure to succeed – and having a mindset of continual improvement to guide your business.

» To perform to the high standard required for sales meeting success, you will need to plan and prepare meticulously.

» You need to use a structured process to build the value of the meeting for both you and the prospect:

   » build your understanding through a call or coffee meeting;

   » send a proposition teaser to build their interest and desire;

   » confirm the meeting to check that the correct people are attending and that all the final details are in place; and

   » print out your building and confirming notes (from your CRM) and take them with you to the meeting along with your notepad .

» The SPQ (Sales Performance Quarters) model is a key tool to help you and your team keep track of time, the key points to cover, and your desired structure for the meeting, so you can concentrate on impressing your potential clients (and making sure your sales meetings do not degenerate into irrelevant chit-chat).

Chapter 7

Performance 2

The First Half of the Meeting

*'Be so good they
can't ignore you.'*

STEVE MARTIN

This second performance chapter will show you how to capitalise on the planning and preparation you've already done, in order to run great sales meetings.

Remember that your potential clients will only buy your product if they like you, trust you and believe that your product will make a big difference. They need to believe that your solution is going to solve a significant challenge they have, and that it is going to add significant value to their organisation. For you to make a sale, they have to be willing to spend money on you, and most businesses only invest if they believe the solution will produce a return on their investment.

To succeed in making a sale or moving to the next stage, you will need to perform superbly in all four quarters of the SPQ model, which we will be exploring over the next two chapters. Believe me, 7/10 will not be good enough for you to become the 'go-to' vendor in your market and consistently make high-value sales. We are looking for a 9/10 or 10/10 performance – that is, close to perfection!

That's my experience of how good we had to be to succeed and how good I believe you need to be to become a scale-up success. The bar for scale-up success is set very high; that's why there are so many start-up failures.

For the rest of this chapter we'll focus on the first two quarters (Qs), and I'll give you the tools to execute the first half of the sales meeting with control and confidence. When you get that right, you will create the platform to perform at your very best in the second half of the meeting.

Before you rush into the meeting

I see a lot of sales people (in fact the majority) rushing into sales meetings, arriving just in time for the start of the meeting without having given themselves time for precise pre-preparation. I believe this is a lazy, complacent approach that will mean they are likely to be on the back foot from the beginning.

Do you think Andrea Bocelli would arrive at the concert hall at the last moment and rush onto the stage? What kind of performance would he give if he did? He might get lucky, but it would be unlikely to be his best performance. Although yours is not a singing performance, you have to perform to the best of your ability to maximise the opportunities the meeting offers and not rely in any way on luck.

To ensure optimum performance in the meeting, I've always used the following 'pre-prep' approach in the run-up to a meeting. Legendary rugby coach Sir Clive Woodward calls these types of activities 'critical non-essentials', and cited them as one of the main reasons England won the Rugby World Cup in 2003.

Top Ten pre-prep tips

1. Prompt pre-prep arrival: arrive near the meeting a *minimum* of one hour before the start time.

2. Coffee shop thinking: find a suitable nearby coffee shop or quiet place to sit down and gather your thoughts.

3. Devices off/Blinkers on: turn off your devices. Don't answer any emails or messages now as they will impair your focus; you need to get your blinkers on.

4. Review notes: recap your notes/objectives for the meeting to gain clarity on what you're trying to achieve.

5. Focus: snap into a focused mindset for the meeting - calm, confident, positive, and friendly.

6. Teamwork: if you're with a colleague, rehearse your roles and how you will work together, so you don't tread on each other's toes.

7. Prompt arrival: ensure you arrive at the client's office a *minimum* of 15–20 minutes before the meeting start time.

8. Advance set-up: ask beforehand if you can go to the meeting room early so you can set up IT/AV before the attendees arrive. There is nothing worse than setting up in front of new prospects and trying to chat while doing so!

9. The right seat: choose a seat that you feel comfortable in, from which you can manage and control the meeting effectively. If there is a beautiful view, do not choose a seat facing it as this may distract you. Also, if there are two or more of you attending, spread out so that you mingle with the other attendees and it doesn't feel like an 'us and them' scenario.

10. Key meeting tools ready: get your notepad, notes and business cards out and your game face on so you're 100% ready to go when they walk in.

These tips may seem basic or obvious, but are you doing them all currently? I guarantee that following them religiously will make a difference to the way you start the meeting and your overall performance in the meeting. They should also become rules of engagement for your sales team to use in every sales meeting situation.

Quarter 1: Rapport

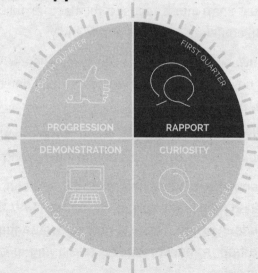

The door opens and the attendees start coming in. What's the most important thing you need to do now? Be calm, be natural, be friendly, and establish rapport.

Whatever else you do in the meeting, it is critical to start by establishing a solid foundation of rapport. If you fail to do this, you will probably perform badly in the meeting. Why is it so important?

Wikipedia superbly sums up the importance of rapport in selling:

> 'Building rapport is one of the most fundamental sales techniques. In sales, rapport is used to build relationships with others quickly and to gain their trust and confidence. It is a very powerful tool that veteran salespeople naturally employ, which allows them to close more deals with less effort.'

Building on this definition, the main reasons you need to establish rapport are:

» People make their minds up quickly – the old cliché that 'first impressions count' is true!

» Rapport is the beginning of building a relationship; without it you're unlikely to be able to move the sale along.

» Your prospects will start to 'like' and 'trust' you – critical components of a strong relationship.

Timings for rapport-building section

As per the SPQ model, this section should take about a quarter of the meeting (Q1 on the diagram). So for a one-hour meeting you would spend 15 minutes from the official start time building rapport before moving on.

Sounds like a lot? Well it is, but it is crucial and the chances are some people will be late, which you should expect and which will eat into your Q1 time anyway. We will also use this quarter to make introductions and start moving the sales conversation forward, so it will not feel too much like 'touchy-feely' chit-chat.

I've seen many sales people over the years open with, 'Good morning everyone, I'm David. We are here today to discuss how we might help your business with… so let's push on with the meeting.' Everyone in the room will be nodding, but without rapport that sales person will be labelled as just another clinical sales person. Not quite what we are looking for or how you want to be seen!

How to develop basic rapport

So how do we develop the all-important basic levels of rapport, while attendees are arriving? It's really quite simple and goes like this:

» Stand up and shake hands warmly (and firmly) with *everyone* who comes into the room, not just the people you regard as the decision-makers. Basic human psychology means bonding with them has now started.

» Chat in a friendly and open way with the people who have arrived until everyone is in the room:

  » some relevant compliments about their organisation that you have found in your research will go down well at this stage; and

  » try not to talk too much about yourself right now, as you want to focus on them by asking natural, open questions (which means they will like you more).

Advanced rapport

Once you've achieved basic rapport you are up and running, but now you need to ramp up the levels of rapport. You can do this in three steps, which should be written down on your notepad as a reminder:

The introductory part of the formal meeting starts with a very brief introduction to you, while you also confidently articulate your proposition from Chapter 1 (2–3 minutes). Also set their expectations on your planned structure for the meeting (1 minute) with words to the effect that before presenting your product you are keen to have an open discussion to find out how they operate and the challenges they face, so you can tailor your presentation to make it relevant. (This scene-setting is important and will buy you time for your questioning, so that they do not become impatient and just expect a pitch or presentation straight away.)

Your second step is an icebreaker (2 minutes): this is a chance for you to stand out from the crowd as someone who is genuinely interested in them. Your icebreaker should be topical, relevant, and provide a natural link to the focus of the meeting (decide on your icebreaker in advance on the basis of your research). An example might be 'I noticed you won a big award for customer service last week – well done! That's great news, because what we're going to discuss today should help you improve even further in this area.' They will appreciate the relevant compliment and you will now make them curious as to how they can get even better.

Thirdly, rapport-building questions (2 minutes): these quick questions will allow you to cement the rapport building you have done so far:

> » 'Before we begin, it would be great to know if there is anything specific you want to get from this meeting?' (It shows you care about them.); and

» 'I appreciate you're all very busy, so can I check how long we've got today, to make sure we use the time wisely?' (Polite and puts you in control, as you then know how much time you have for each section of your SPQ model).

End of Q1

That's it for Q1. Getting this right is not quite as easy as it sounds, so it's worth challenging yourself and your team, and tightening up on the areas mentioned. My belief is that to build strong rapport, you should above all else just be yourself – natural, authentic, and modest – and people will like, respect and trust you.

But it's also critical that your time management in Q1 is impeccable, so keep a close eye on the clock. The timings specified above should take you to just over ten minutes, which gives you a five-minute buffer to allow for any late arrivals or unexpected delays. If you over-run on Q1, you risk losing control of the whole meeting, as the other quarters will start losing their shape and structure.

If you feel you've covered the key rapport-building in less time than planned, then feel free to move on to Q2.

Quarter 2: Curiosity

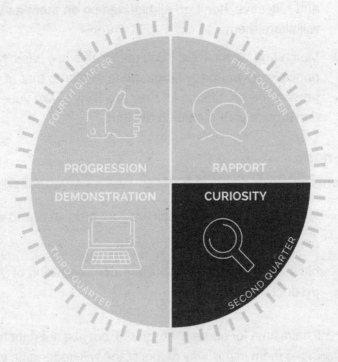

So you're now into Q2. If it's a one-hour meeting, you are 15 minutes in and you're off to a good start. You've built a good connection in the room, which means you're getting on well with the attendees.

You're about to move into a new stage, but it's important to keep building the rapport throughout Q2 and the rest of the meeting by using these three tips:

» Know and use their language, so they feel as if you understand their world (for example, if you are selling to a law firm you will gain brownie points for using specific law firm language such as 'fee earners', 'support staff' and 'back office').

» Tailor your level of energy to theirs: if they appear quiet and reflective, don't go all high tempo on them as you will scare them.

» Match and mirror – but don't mimic: this is a basic NLP principle; if your body language is similar to that of the person you are talking to, they are likely to like you, but don't make your matching obvious.

No-nos

So what do you do now to kick off Q2? Well, what you *don't* do is:

» tell them at length how brilliant your product is and why

» present a PowerPoint slide show

» blow them away with a brilliant demonstration of your product

You will have time for some of this in Q3, but just not right now, as selling to them in this way at this stage will undermine your credibility and make you look 'salesy'.

Equally, the potential client may ask you at this stage to explain more about your product. Don't fall into the trap of pitching your product right now, as you will lose control of the meeting. Give them a brief and polite answer in line with your proposition, and then refocus.

Using curiosity to find their pain points

The key objective in Q2 is to use your curiosity skills to uncover their key challenges (or pain points). We explored curiosity in detail in Chapter 2. Remember that curiosity is being genuinely interested in the people you are talking to. The easiest way to demonstrate curiosity is by asking intelligent questions and listening carefully to the answers.

So why do we need to ask a bunch of questions at this stage? Well, good questions will get your prospects to articulate that they have a need or want for your product. It makes presenting your proposition in Q3 much easier if they've already characterised themselves as likely to gain benefit from your product.

How to be curious

The exact questions to ask will depend on the type of product you are selling, the market you are selling into, and the type of meeting. However, the four main principles of good questioning are similar for all meetings:

» Ask open questions – about their thoughts or opinions, so you can hear what they really think (as opposed to a closed question, to which they can just answer 'yes' or 'no').

» Listen – this is a critical selling skill that many sales people don't deploy well. When you have asked a question, sit back, listen carefully, and note down the key points. You will be gathering information about specific needs and people will be impressed that you are listening carefully and taking notes.

» Probe – this is a key component of curiosity. Good probing will enable you to drill down to uncover tangible needs and challenges with deeper questioning after someone has given a first answer. (I've given some examples of good probing questions below.)

» Take notes – unless you have a photographic memory (be honest with yourself about this); precise note-taking is essential to capture the key points, while also keeping eye contact and control of the conversation. (you'll get better at this the more you do it)

Good questions for uncovering challenges and needs

I have limited scope in this book to cover the range of questions you should ask. However, there are whole books written on this topic. Professor Neil Rackham, whom I had the pleasure of meeting when he flew to London to do a superb keynote speech for us a few years ago, wrote the highly rated *SPIN Selling,*[1] which presents what is still a great methodology for questioning in sales. SPIN focuses on a four-level model for asking questions and eliciting needs: **S**ituation, **P**roblem, **I**mplication, **N**eed. Although SPIN is focused primarily on large companies, the principles of questioning are still similar.

For now, here are some very simple themes, to get you thinking about your ideal set of questions:

» Ask questions to reveal their needs and wants: 'Are there any areas you feel you need to improve on?'

» Identify pains and problems: 'What are the biggest challenges you face?'

» Highlight challenges: play back to them the challenges they have mentioned and get them to articulate the value of solving these problems.

» Understand aspirations: eliciting information about aspirational needs can be a powerful technique, as it will get them thinking about something they have always dreamed of – 'In an ideal world what would you like to be able to offer your clients in this area?'

---

1   Neil Rackham, *Spin Selling*, Gower Publishing 1995.

Uncovering needs

Questioning based on the excellent themes above will start identifying some challenges and needs. If members of the meeting give answers like, 'Yes, communicating with our clients is a major challenge for us' and your product helps with communication, you have started to uncover a need that your product may satisfy.

You would then want to probe more, to find out precisely what the communication challenge is. The more specific you can get when uncovering needs, the better. If you can identify more than one strong need, that is great news as it will give you different angles to sell your product (they may reject one of the 'needs' or say that it is not that important) and therefore improve your chances of making a sale.

Best practice in uncovering pain points and needs

I started my career in sales in the pharmaceutical industry, with AstraZeneca, where I sold to GPs and top consultants. I was also privileged to view some live consultations between doctors and patients, as part of AZ's ongoing research.

I have to say that in terms of a best practice template of curiosity, good questioning, probing and uncovering pain points and needs, some of these top consultants were incredible – far better than any sales person I have ever seen. They started with great open questions and listened carefully, probing to find out specific details about the problem; then, after a series of intelligent questions, they produced a clear diagnosis of what they thought the problem was and a recommended solution. Top lawyers perform at a similar level of excellence.

This is the same technique as finding out pain points in sales. These professionals have mastered the art of asking questions in a professional, probing manner that gets to the heart of the problem, but politely and respectfully, so that it does not feel too intrusive. This is exactly the type of behaviour that you and your team need to model and practise in order to become brilliant at uncovering needs and challenges.

End of Q2 (and the first half)

You're now at the end of the second quarter of the meeting and therefore halfway through. If all has gone to plan, you will have:

» established excellent rapport with all the attendees

» asked some excellent open questions, without getting people's backs up or losing any rapport

» uncovered at least one key challenge or need, possibly more

» managed your time precisely, so that in a one-hour meeting you are no more than 30 minutes through (if you over-run, the second half of the meeting will be a rush)

If you can achieve the above, you will have done incredibly well. In the short span of 30 minutes or so, you will have established a solid platform on which to base a strong perfor-mance in the second half of the meeting.

Summary

Q1: Rapport

» Make the pre-prep top ten tips part of your sales team's rules of engagement, to be used in every sales meeting.

» Establish basic rapport until all the attendees are in the room.

» Upgrade to advanced rapport using three easy steps:

> » an introduction, incorporating your proposition and setting expectations on the format of the meeting
>
> » a relevant and impressive icebreaker
>
> » asking rapport-building questions to cement trust and respect

» Finish Q1 bang on time or slightly before (i.e., a quarter of the way through the meeting)

Q2: Curiosity

» Use curiosity to uncover their key challenges, pain points and needs, using four main principles:

> » ask open questions
>
> » listen
>
> » probe
>
> » take concise notes

» Devise a list of good questions relevant to your target clients for uncovering challenges and needs, and make sure your team also use them.

» You can always improve at expressing your curiosity, which is a critical component of good selling. Model your behaviour on that of the best doctors and lawyers.

» Effective time management of Q2 should ensure that the end of the first half of the meeting arrives at 30 minutes (or slightly less) into a one-hour meeting.

Chapter 8

Performance 3
The Second Half of The Meeting

'If you don't see yourself as a winner, then you cannot perform as a winner.'

ZIG ZIGLAR

You are now into the second half of the meeting. You have laid the foundations and now you need to pick up the pace and use your passion to persuade the attendees that your product can solve their challenges. Once you have impressed them with your demonstration or presentation, you then need to gain their commitment to proceed and a plan to progress.

Quarter 3: Demonstration

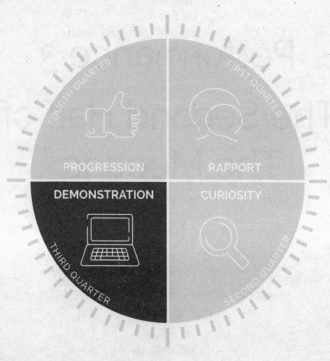

Quarter 3 is where you should start visually showcasing your product and linking its benefits to their needs. You have two options for this: a presentation or a demonstration. You can use either, but don't forget that in a one-hour meeting you will only have around 15 minutes for this section. My strong personal preference, especially if you're selling a technology product, is to do a demonstration.

Death by PowerPoint

So why do I recommend a demonstration? A good presentation can be effective, but let's be honest, it could come across as death by PowerPoint. We've all been there many times, mentally scarred from attending so many dry, dull PowerPoint presentations. In fact, around the world 30 million PowerPoint presentations are given every day.[1] Much has been written on the need to use new presenting options instead of PowerPoint, but the majority of suggestions are still similar: slide-based visual tools (Keynote, Slides, Prezi, SlideRocket, Easel.ly, Emaze, Slidedog, to name but a few).

Even if your presentation is good, many people will still switch into 'power save' mode when you start flicking through the slides and you may well lose control of the meeting. And here's another thing to consider - if you start presenting, you will create a feeling that you are 'the sales person' and they are 'the prospect'.

Having worked so hard in the first half of the meeting to build up great rapport, you don't want to undo your good work and create distance between you and the audience. Leave presentations to corporate people. As an entrepreneurial company, you can be braver and more memorable than this!

Demonstration brings your product to life

I've done many presentations and demonstrations over the years, and from my experience it is much more powerful to do a technology demonstration. Showcasing your software interface by pointing and clicking through the key benefits (using your mouse/cursor) directly from your laptop screen (ideally linked to a big screen) is a 'live' performance, which should keep your audience interested and engaged.

A demonstration has several advantages:

» it enables you to bring your proposition to life visually

» it shows the actual product they would be buying and

---

1   Quora.com, 2014.

gives the attendees clarity and confidence as to what it looks and feels like (slides just don't give this effect and can appear evasive)

» it provides tangible evidence that you can help solve their problems or satisfy their needs and wants

» it enables you to demonstrate mastery of your own product (which will impress the audience)

» it's your opportunity to match their needs and challenges with your solution by tailoring your demonstration to address the pain points they will have mentioned in Q2

It's not easy to do a demonstration well, and you need to be brave and bold to take it on and do so successfully – which is why a lot of people don't do it well, or don't do it at all! But this creates an opportunity for you to make a real impact and differentiate yourself from the rest of your competitors, many of whom will play it safe with PowerPoint presentations.

If you're selling a product you don't think demonstrates well, or you're selling multiple products or a portfolio of solutions, doing a demonstration with just one of your solutions may not work. In that case I'd still recommend getting visual and interactive as by this stage in the meeting (after a lot of Q&A in the first half), you need to ramp up the energy levels. As an example, you could jump up and start using a whiteboard or a flipchart, doing some drawings of concepts that will stimulate interest, opinions and engaged conversation. You'll win respect from the attendees for being brave enough to do this and they'll welcome the visual variety, which will help to balance out the four quarters of the meeting.

Creating the magic for a demo that wows

So let's explore how to prepare and practise a demonstration that will give your prospects a desire for your product and the confidence to buy it. (We will assume that you have a technology product, so refer back to the suggestions above if you have another sort of product).

How do you create this world-class demonstration? One thing is for sure, unless you're a genius, you're very unlikely to be able to just walk into the meeting and wing it!

The demo is at the very heart of all the selling you do. It needs to be expertly designed, carefully built, and practised religiously until you achieve perfection. It's a simple equation, which I've experienced personally: if your demo is brilliant, people will believe in you, your product and your company, and the resulting sales will drive a rapid scale-up!

The following are the foundation points of a really effective demo:

» knowing the primary pain points of your target customers and structuring a demo around how your product solves those problems

» identifying the top ten features/benefits of your product that will make an immediate impact within your Q3 time (and not bore the meeting attendees) and focusing on those key benefits

Top Eight demo tips

So how do we craft a demo that is high-impact, relevant, and inspiring? The first thing to remember is that in a one-hour meeting you only have 15 minutes for this section – not enough time to do an A-Z tour of all the features of your product.

Less is definitely more in a good demo, so to keep it sharp and concise use the following tips.

1. Focus only on the key benefits for your prospects (to a maximum of ten).

2. Make your product look easy to use, so they can imagine adopting and using the product easily, both personally and as a firm. (Sales people often feel the need to make their product look sophisticated and complicated, but that just confuses potential customers.)

3. Vary your demo to show different user experiences; if you have sales people, management and IT in the room you will score points if you illustrate the product from each user perspective.

4. Use passion to create emotion and desire: sometimes when you've got your head down 'demo-ing', your person-ality may go missing without you realising. Remember, this is your opportunity to show off your product!

5. Turn product features into benefits, by using the phrase 'which means that': for example, 'clicking this button drops a list of visitors to your website (feature), *which means that* you can identify new prospects and contact them directly to book a sales meeting' (benefit).

6. Emphasise the return on investment (ROI): the company you are meeting will only buy your product if they believe it will produce a return on their investment. It's not easy, but you have to give them the evidence as to how and why this would happen. (Bringing in some high-impact sound bites from relevant clients on savings or increased revenue is a good way to do this.)

7. Finish with a concise summary of benefits. You'd think this would be an obvious thing to do, but many people forget this. It is critical for cleanly positioning and cementing the benefits of your product in your potential client's mind.

8. Last, but definitely not least, once you have crafted your demo devise a script for you and your team. Yes, a

script – otherwise your team will waffle and warble. A script ensures you all neatly encapsulate what you're showing on the screen.

A great demo in one day

So is that it? Having understood the prerequisites for a good demo and started to draft your very own demo using the top eight tips, are you ready to get out there and start selling with it? Not quite yet... you now need to refine and practise your demo so that by the time you get in front of potential customers you know it inside out and back to front!

Here's a ten-point plan I've always used to develop, refine and practise great demos. This plan will pull everything together and get you ready to impress prospects.

1. Build and practise as a team: building a demo from scratch, or revising one, and practising it together will be a great bonding experience for your team (allow a full day of focused, quality time for this).

2. Brainstorm a draft script together for the first hour of the day, using the key points you have noted down from the 'Creating the magic' and 'Top Eight demo tips' sections above).

3. Lead from the front: to test the draft script offer to do the first demo direct from your laptop linked to a big screen (offering to step up will gain you respect), then ask for open and honest feedback at the end.

4. Take turns, with everyone doing a first demo (with no interruptions) and capturing all constructive feedback on a flip chart along the way.

5. Review and refine the demo/script in line with the most common feedback from the demo practice sessions.

6. Repeat all of the above until everyone in the team is feeling extremely confident with the overall flow and structure of the demo.

7. Run real-life 'role-play' demos in which the rest of the sales team play potential customers in a meeting situation – throwing in objections, interrupting the presenter, being difficult, etc. (use a stopwatch to check the timings in line with the SPQ model timings.)

8. These role-play sessions may act as a reality check, indicating that a lot of practice is still needed to run a perfect demo under time and peer pressure!

9. Go for lunch, come back in the afternoon, and practise, practise, practise until the end of the day.

10. At the end of the day, congratulate everyone on a fantastic effort and take them down the pub for some well-earned drinks. I guarantee they will be fully pumped (albeit exhausted!), ready to start demo-ing tomorrow.

We did a world-class demo practice day at BigHand when we brought out a long-awaited new version of our product. There was plenty of blood, sweat and tears in a full-day session like this, but the team never forgot the day. The atmosphere, the open and honest dialogue, the ultimate professionalism for a small company, and the bonding between colleagues created an ethos of teamwork and loyalty for a long time afterwards.

And the best thing is that when you next sit with one of your team in a sales meeting, you will feel very proud of their performance.

Quarter 4: Progression

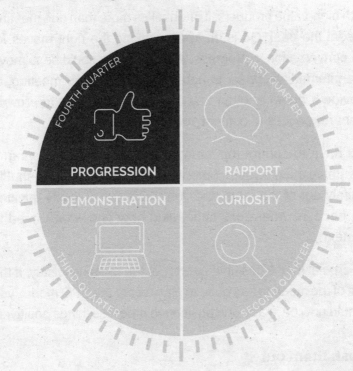

You've now got your perfect demo (or almost perfect, as it will continue to get better). Remember that when you run this in a meeting situation, you need to finish this section exactly three quarters of the way through the meeting, in line with the SPQ model. There is no room for drift on this, because if you do over-run on your demo, or on any of the other sections, you will eat into Q4 time.

But you may be thinking that surely Q4 is just a nice wrap-up, saying your goodbyes, unplugging your laptop, etc. Far from it. Q4 is a critical quarter and it pulls together all your hard work from the rest of the meeting.

Quarter 4 is all about progression.

What is progression?

With high-value products, it often takes more than one meeting to seal the deal. Q4 is all about making the right moves for the conversation to progress. A progression could be to move to an immediate close, to agree to have another meeting, to provide a demo to other key decision makers, or to provide client references to cement your credibility.

You have to control the situation expertly by suggesting or assuming the next step, otherwise your prospects will shuffle politely out of the room and you'll be left helplessly thinking 'I'm not sure where this is heading now and what I need to do next... '

It's crucial to use this final quarter of the meeting wisely. If the rest of the meeting has gone to plan as per the SPQ model, you should now be in a strong position to progress things positively.

Flush them out

During the demo, in Q3, you have been doing a lot of the talking, without the attendees talking much. Now you need to get them talking again, to find out what they really think. Do they like your product? Are they convinced by your company? Are they confused? Do they have concerns?

To flush out concerns and deal with honest feedback, the two best techniques are:

» Curiosity: it's time to get curious again, to uncover their real opinions. You don't just want them to be polite; you want to draw out what they really think and where you stand. You now understand the principles of curiosity, so I'll leave it to you to compile the best open questions for your business. A good simple starter for after the demo is 'So, it would be great to hear your initial thoughts on our product.'

» Objection handling: as part of your curiosity questioning you will hear some positives and some negatives. If you do not hear any concerns, probe deeper, as it's likely that people are just being polite. It's important to uncover their concerns and handle these objections to make sure they are still on board.

   » The key to handling objections is viewing objections as positive, as it means the attendees have bothered to voice a concern. This normally means they are interested in your product. Take it as a positive buying signal.

   » A good way to handle an objection is to be calm, empathise with the question and ask a question back to clarify what they mean, for example, 'That's an excellent question, could you explain exactly what it is about the interface that you are concerned about?' This approach means you will not appear reactive or defensive, and it also buys you some time to think about a good answer.

Three progression routes

'What do you think would be a good way to move this forward?'

This is a great question to ask to set up the progression discussion. The last thing you want to do now is to start acting like a sales person and make them feel you are pressurising them and trying to close them down. You don't want to undo all the good work from the rest of the meeting. By asking this intelligent, open question, you put the ball firmly in their court and they will respect this.

Their answer will show you how positive they are feeling about moving forward. You don't have to go with their exact response as it may be vague, but you could politely 'counter-answer' and suggest any of the following three most likely progression routes:

Sale: if it's obvious they are fully convinced and want to proceed, why not gain their commitment and suggest moving the project forward?

» Offer to email them an order form or get them to sign a hard copy there and then, and also suggest your project manager contacts them to start scheduling the project. (Fast closes like this are more likely with SME companies and small order values.)

» The order form should have a simple set of terms and conditions attached to it, which they sign up to. There is no point in getting bogged down with full contracts; they can come later. For now, you just need to close the sale!

Proposal: your prospects are often quite likely to ask for a proposal. This is a particular bugbear of mine, as I've seen sales people waste hour after hour creating proposals when it's obvious they have no chance of making the sale! From your curiosity probing, you will now have a good feel for whether they are genuinely interested in moving forward.

» If you feel they are not really interested, there is absolutely no point in putting together any proposal. Even if they ask for one, politely suggest that you will send them a detailed 'information summary pack': a classy piece of pre-prepared promotional collateral that you can ping off with a polite cover email in a matter of minutes.

» If you feel they are interested, proactively offer a short, sharp executive summary proposal of a handful of pages.

People normally like this as everyone is time-poor nowadays and this will also save you time. It goes without saying you should have pre-loaded templates you can swiftly edit and send soon after the meeting.

Book a meeting from a meeting: this was one of the key sales mantras of a former colleague of mine and it is a good one! If you think that they are genuinely interested but you realise you are not going to close them quickly, you have to accept that you're going to require more stages to close the sale.

» If you can get them to commit to the next meeting now, you're getting yourself back in for more face-to-face contact to build the relationship. Further meetings are likely to be with other decision makers, for example, members of the board, the management team, the technology team, etc.

» Follow-up meetings with other decision makers should still use the SPQ model for their core structure, though you may want to tweak the shape and timings slightly, for example, by allowing less time for Q2 (curiosity), as by now you should know most of their challenges and needs.

Prospect procrastination

Be aware that even if you have had a good meeting and followed all the advice above, the easiest course of action (progression) for the potential client is to procrastinate and say, 'Well, thanks very much for that, let us have a think and get back to you.' This happens all the time and is a standard response, so don't panic!

Without further information, this leaves you in the dark and not in control of the progression of the sales conversation. If this situation occurs, remain calm, use your curiosity skills and (depending on their responses) suggest one of the progression routes mentioned above.

You don't want to appear 'pushy', but you may need to be assertive, challenging and persuasive to gain some sort of commitment to move to the next stage. These are not easy skills, but they are key sales skills for you and your team to use and practise over time, so that you come across as driven, passionate and assertive, rather than pushy or aggressive.

As you've already built a good rapport with them, if you revert to asking curious questions (rather than telling them what to do) and persuade them using your passion, you will normally succeed in gaining some sort of commitment to the next stage (even if it's a commitment to speak on the phone next week at the same time).

But don't push them so hard that you fall out with them! Any movement forward is progress.

SPQ Model

So you've now finished Q4 and the meeting has ended. If you've followed the sales performance quarters (SPQ) model, the chances are you will have had a great meeting.

Although we obviously all strive for perfection, not all meetings will be perfect, as there are so many different, 'live', variables at work, some of which are outside our control. However, the structure and focus of the SPQ model will enable you to give your absolute best in every meeting and maximise the opportunities within the time available:

> » By building strong rapport in Q1 you start to develop a relationship with the attendees, so that they begin to like and trust you.

» Building on the rapport you have established, in Q2 you will subtly use your curiosity skills to ask the right questions for finding out their key needs, challenges and pain points.

» You will then run a superb demonstration in Q3 to inspire and excite your prospects and illustrate how your product can solve their challenges, add value, and create a remarkable return on investment for their business.

» Q4 is the progression quarter, where you pull the meeting together, find out what everyone really thinks, and then propose a plan to move the conversation forward towards a successful sale.

I know from experience that using this simple model will allow you, as the leader, to take control of the sales meeting process. And, much like sports coaches making sure their players are match fit, with the SPQ model you can ensure that your sales people are 'meeting fit' at all times, and trust that they will perform in a disciplined, high-quality and consistent way. When you get your team's performance in sales meetings absolutely right, the rate at which you make sales will ensure that your scale-up gathers pace and momentum.

The even better news is that the structure and professionalism of the model will mean your clients will like the way you sell to them, which will increase your chances of making sales. I'd encourage you to put this SPQ model right at the core of your sales process and revisit, refine and practise it as often as possible.

Summary

Q3: Demonstration

» Use a demonstration rather than a presentation to bring your product to life and give your prospects clarity and confidence in what they would be buying.

» Draft and build your demo using the foundation points and the Top Eight demo tips.

» Create, refine and practise 'a great demo in one day' using the practical ten-point plan.

» At sales meetings, always finish Q3 on schedule (that is, three quarters of the way through the meeting), to allow time for structured, professional progression in Q4.

Q4: Progression

» Progression is a critical quarter (not just saying your goodbyes) and you must use the time effectively.

» Flush out objections by expertly using your curiosity skills.

» Decide on a feasible progression route (depending on feedback) and gain commitment in a confident, decisive manner.

» If they're positive and keen, don't be afraid to ask for the business and close the sale by offering to send an order form and getting your project manager to provisionally book out time to start the project.

» Time management of all four quarters should ensure that the meeting finishes bang on time or slightly early – you'll always get brownie points for an early finish.

Chapter 9
Precision

*'If I had eight hours to
chop down a tree, I'd spend
six sharpening my axe.'*

ABRAHAM LINCOLN

In the book so far we've looked at five of the six key areas (the six Ps described in the Introduction) to focus on, in order to scale up your business through sales. Each section on its own should help you improve, and when combined should provide you with a strong process to strengthen your overall sales performance.

However, there is one more key step to cover to complete the 6-Step Scale Up Process and enhance your overall scale-up pace and performance. This area is a crucial one, but in the frenzied pursuit of sales growth in a fast-moving entrepreneurial business it is often overlooked.

The sixth P is precision.

What is precision?

So what is precision? The dictionary definition is a good start: 'Precision - the quality, condition or fact of being exact and accurate.'

To bring this definition to life, let's take a look at some examples of what precision might look like in the world at large:

» For astronaut Tim Peake precision could be the precise second at which he must return from his space walk and re-enter the European space station before his oxygen runs out.

» For singer Katherine Jenkins precision might be hitting the final note in the right key at exactly the right moment.

» For car company Jaguar Land Rover precision could be a robot laser cutting metal for a chassis to the accuracy of one thousandth of a millimetre.

Legendary computer scientist Niklaus Wirth emphasised the importance of precision in the technology world with this astute observation:

> 'But quality of work can be expected only through personal satisfaction, dedication and enjoyment. In our profession, precision and perfection are not a dispensable luxury, but a simple necessity.'

The difference that makes the difference

The above-named people certainly believe that precision is critical, and in their worlds there is very little margin for error. But how important is precision for you as an entrepreneur?

In terms of scaling up your business, implementing the other five Ps in this book could make you successful, but a lack of precision creates risks that you might perhaps be a bit too scattergun, make too many mistakes and possibly not be focused enough to become successful. And why would you take risks with the scale-up of your business and ultimately the pursuit of your entrepreneurial dreams?

Many top business people believe there is a fine line between success and failure in business – a sentiment I've always agreed with. In fact, I've always seen precision as the difference that makes the difference: a perfectionist mindset that can markedly improve your chances of scale-up success.

Another way of looking at it is that by focusing on the other five Ps you will create a solid sales engine to drive your scale-up, and precision could be seen as the turbocharger to power up the speed of your sales growth.

In this chapter we will investigate what precision in scale-up selling looks like and how it can benefit you.

Precision in scale-up sales

As I mentioned in Chapter 6, our top sports stars and teams are always striving to improve performance through 'the aggregation of marginal gains'. Their precision lies in seeking tiny percentage point improvements in everything they do to make a cumulative difference to overall performance and results.

Precision in scale-up selling is a similar concept: if you and your team operate with accuracy, quality and precision in everything you do, you will continually make improvements, and better performance and sales results will follow. Being precise is hard work to start with (most things in business are!), but once you get the hang of it, it becomes a habit like any other and will pay back handsomely.

So, let's look in more detail at what precision means for our other five Ps of scale-up to illustrate how you can strive for perfection in each element of your sales process.

Precision for your proposition

As we've explored already in Chapter 1, the proposition is at the core of everything you do in your scale-up selling. Before we examine a precise proposition, it's worth mentioning that from my experience of witnessing many poor, imprecise propositions, I'd recommend that you should avoid the following:

- » putting up a slide of a map of the world with dots on it and saying 'we work in 57 countries...' – this comes across as arrogant and irrelevant

- » mentioning a list of client names as part of your core proposition – this is trying too hard; prospects will expect you to be working with decent clients

- » rambling on pompously for a few minutes about how great your business is and exactly what you do, when all the potential client wants is a brief snapshot – this will tarnish any rapport you have built

So, to construct and deliver a precise proposition and instantly differentiate yourself from rambling, overconfident competitors:

- » use simple, precise language (no waffle!)

- » don't include client names as part of your core proposition – these can come later, when the prospect asks for client examples, which is when they will sound more impressive and less like bragging

» remember that less is more – never expand on your core proposition, as it's more impressive to reveal benefits about yourself over time as the sales conversation unfolds

» use the clear communications techniques recommended by expert author Andy Bounds.[1] I know Andy well and he is a guru of precision in sales communications:

  » One of Andy's key tools is AFTERs. As he explains, the key to good selling is always to focus on the AFTERs, i.e. why the other party will be better off after they have used your product.

  » So don't talk about your product ('we sell exceptional websites'), but focus on the AFTERs it delivers ('we can help you stand out from the crowd, improve your lead generation and help you make more sales.')

Precision in your passion

You would think that all passion is great! Well, passion is nearly always great, and believe me I'm one of its biggest fans! But there is a danger of overdoing it and sounding 'salesy', so here are some pointers to harnessing your passion with precision.

Be precise with when you use passion in sales conversations. Examples of when to turn on the passion are:

» when explaining your proposition

» when you're doing your demonstration

» when someone asks you why you are better than your competitors

---

1   Andy Bounds, andyboundsonline.com.

Be precise with the language you use when you become passionate and beware of using too many superlatives when talking about your product, for example, 'amazing', 'unique', 'incredible', 'unbelievable' (prospects may become wary and start thinking 'this sounds too good to be true.') Precise, sincere language works more effectively, especially if you use phrases such as:

» 'I'm extremely proud of the product we have created specifically for this market... '

» 'Our research study has shown that businesses like you generate a strong return on investment from using our technology... '

» 'As a business, we genuinely want to make a difference by... '

Precision in building your pipeline

As we established in Chapter 4, building a strong pipeline is critical for being able to scale up your business quickly. Precision is a critical component for a solid, sustainable pipeline, and I'd recommend you focus on two key areas to start with:

Precise targeting: as we saw in Chapter 4, many entrepreneurial firms take a 'we'll sell to anyone as long as it grows sales revenue' approach. It's true that this will grow sales revenue, but it is an inefficient route to long-term, sustainable growth. The best way to create a dynamic, sustainable pipeline is to target with precision. Identify your client target niche and stick with it. If you want to target more precisely, you can even fine-tune it into a 'micro niche'.

As an example, you might identify your target niche as financial services, then distil this down to professional financial services, then to accountancy firms, then to SME accountancy firms with up to 500 employees. By focusing on this micro niche you will get known, gain word-of-mouth recommendations, and grow sales quickly. Do the maths on market size, but there could be millions of pounds of sales for your company within this micro niche alone! And once you dominate a micro niche you can start growing back up into the larger 'parent' niche.

Micro niche

```
┌─────────────────────────────────┐
│                                 │
│       Financial Services        │
│                                 │
└─────────────────────────────────┘
                 ↓
┌─────────────────────────────────┐
│          Professional           │
│       Financial Services        │
│                                 │
└─────────────────────────────────┘
                 ↓
┌─────────────────────────────────┐
│                                 │
│       Accountancy Firms         │
│                                 │
└─────────────────────────────────┘
                 ↓
┌─────────────────────────────────┐
│         SME Accountancy         │
│      Firms < 500 Employees      │
│                                 │
└─────────────────────────────────┘
```

Precise pipeline management: firms always start building their pipeline with a lot of excitement and enthusiasm, but over time sloppiness can kick in, which can impair the probability of converting leads into sales. CRM is at the core of your sales and marketing activities, and this is where precision is extremely important. Set up best practice rules for the CRM for everyone in sales and marketing. You need to be super-strict on this as your people may be complacent with CRM. Rules to cover include:

» accuracy of data entry (typos, blank fields, etc. are not acceptable)

» categorising prospects precisely and logging them as, for example, hot, warm or cold (this is also important for targeting/segmenting your marketing)

» a requirement for sales people to log precise meeting notes by the end of each week (critical for precision in follow-up and closing)

» the responsibility of sales people to manage, clean and update their pipelines regularly to ensure accurate sales data. It is crucial for you as a leader to be able to run CRM reports with precise sales forecast data at any given point in time.

Precision for your people

To create a world-class team (yes, it is possible in a small firm!) and make sure they remain focused and motivated, it is critical that you apply precision in leading your people. Key areas to focus on include:

» a precise definition of your sales culture, to ensure your team have absolute clarity on the culture, the vision and exactly what is expected of them. (Post it on your sales team wall – virtually as well, if possible – and high performance will follow.)

» precision in your leadership:

» it's critical for you to be clear, consistent and precise in your oral and email communications with your people; inconsistency and imprecision can breed unrest, confusion and demotivation.

» coaching: identify with precision which particular aspects of performance you feel they can improve on, and identify clear, specific performance targets to work towards, which you should review regularly.

» precision in developing your recognition and rewards scheme: it's a tricky area, but when you get this right, it will be a huge motivator. You need a clear, structured scheme that is fair, aspirational and as good as any big company can offer.

» be precise in the definitions and rules for hitting targets, as targets and money will understandably always be emotional areas – for example, if someone ends up at 99.5% of target will you round this up and pay out a bonus, or is the rule people must be at 100 % or above?

» do your research and involve your own sales team in a brainstorming session to develop the ultimate reward programme – this will mean they are fully motivated and do not moan about it!

» a precision sales toolkit for you and your team: in my experience relatively little thought goes into the very tools that you will be using for day-to-day selling! As a nimble, entrepreneurial business you have the freedom to create clever tools to surprise and delight your prospects. It should be an evolving list, but examples I've found that work well include:

» slick animated videos showcasing your customers' pain points and how your product solves them (Videoscribe by Sparkol is a super video tool)

> » surprisingly short, snappy and easy-to-read promo-
>   tional material (A5 handouts)

> » cool, classy, highly-branded business cards that
>   make a statement (first impressions count and are
>   worth paying for)

Precision for performance

We've already explored in detail in Chapters 6–8 how performance in sales meetings is one of the key success factors for
your overall scale-up success. In those chapters we looked
at many specific examples of precision for performance, so
for now I only want to give an example of the importance of
precision to be able to move the sales conversation towards
closing the sale. Closing is the natural result of a good sales
process, but in order to close effectively, your performance
in all four quarters of the SPQ model needs to be packed full
of precision.

I was once fortunate enough to find myself at 10 Downing Street
in a large, daunting boardroom, selling software to a group of
prospects that included the Prime Minister's wife. I followed
the structure and timings of the SPQ model, which gave me a
good, solid platform to perform well, even though I was under
intense pressure. Things generally went well, but there were
a few crunch moments that stick in my mind, as they clearly
demonstrated the importance of precision in ensuring that the
meeting moved in the right direction.

Early on in Q1 (rapport), someone tried to hurry things along
by saying 'OK, can we get on with the demo, please?' I had to
respond politely that we would get to the demo but that first it was
important to discuss the way they worked and the challenges
they had, otherwise the demo wouldn't really make sense. By

standing my ground on this, I was ensuring that I stuck to the precise structure and timings (as well as gaining respect).

In Q2 (curiosity), as I'd sensed in Q1 that they seemed in a hurry, I cut down my curiosity questioning to just three very precise questions. This still gave me enough information to proceed to Q3 with confidence, while making the attendees feel I was moving the meeting along at a good pace.

I knew I had to get Q3 (demonstration) spot on to impress them enough to move forward. I had researched and practised in advance, focusing on precision in the language I would use during the demo, to make them feel I understood their world. Because I was precise with my language, the attendees tuned into what I was saying and the demo section led perfectly to setting up Q4.

In Q4 (progression) I had flushed out and handled a couple of objections and then tried to close the sale by suggesting a minimum five-user project. We went round the room and drummed up four volunteers, and then, after a few no's, we reached the last potential volunteer, who happened to be the Prime Minister's wife. I asked her if she would like to be one of the users of the software. She paused for about 10 seconds, deep in thought, and then said, 'No'. I was obviously disappointed, but I didn't panic; I just used curiosity questioning to find out her reasons.

After ascertaining some key facts, including her main objection of being time-poor, I proposed that we train her in the 10 Downing Street private flat for three one-hour sessions in the afternoon, before she picked up the kids from school – not our standard model, but as an entrepreneurial business I was able to offer a flexible, precisely tailored, plan that would suit her. By doing this, I managed to make her feel comfortable and valued.

The order form came through later that day. A proud, confidence-building moment for our small, ambitious business!

Precision makes the difference

So you can see that precision is about quality, accuracy, marginal gains and having a growth mindset of continually trying to improve, and ultimately striving for perfection.

I have only covered a few examples in this chapter, and you can obviously use precision to improve in a multitude of ways. But the point is that if you make a precision mindset an integral part of your sales culture, it will complement and boost the other five Ps and will enable you to build a superb reputation by continually exceeding client and prospect expectations.

For this to work, though, you need a high-quality, hungry and eager sales team who thrive on the challenge of trying to get better every day. So ensure you embed precision into your sales culture, so that your people don't see this 'perfectionism' as a negative, but as a 100% positive philosophy. When they believe that, you will have created a driven, high-performance culture to move you towards scale-up success.

Summary

» Precision is the difference that makes the difference – a perfectionist mindset that can turbocharge the speed of your scale-up.

» Embed a precision mindset into your sales culture, so that your people want to try to get better every day. Involve your people by regularly asking them, 'How do you think we can get better?'

» Put together a list of relevant, practical ways in which your business could bring more precision to the other five Ps, and update it regularly as part of your culture of continual improvement.

Chapter 10

Time to Take Action

'Faith is taking the first step even when you can't see the whole staircase.'

MARTIN LUTHER KING JR

As we near the end of *Scale Up Millionaire*, I hope that you have found the book interesting, informative and inspirational. I also hope that the scale-up process that we've explored comes across as practical, easy-to-use and achievable.

In an ideal world, I'd love to come and get stuck in personally to help you achieve your dreams, but in reality this book should offer you the support you need, with ideas, insights, a solid process and, most importantly, the confidence to go out and give it everything you've got to get exactly what you want.

We've covered a lot of ground in a short space of time, exploring:

» why most current start-ups fail, and why successful scale-up of entrepreneurial businesses has become a key strategic objective for the government and the business community – which means you're going to be part of a new, exciting wave of fast-growth scale-up businesses keen to make a difference;

» why selling will make the biggest difference to your successful scale-up, by enabling you to drive your own growth, retain control along the journey, and exit on your own terms;

» the common myths, excuses and barriers related to selling, to give you a focused mindset for successful scale-up through sales;

» an easy-to-use, logical, practical model involving a proven 6-Step Scale Up Process:

  » Proposition
  » Passion
  » Pipeline
  » People
  » Performance
  » Precision

» how to use the Sales Performance Quarters (SPQ) model to ensure you and your team perform to the best of your ability in every sales meeting (these crunch meetings will ultimately determine your sales success and the speed of your scale-up);

» how to overcome the challenges of scaling up successfully by adopting a precision mindset to complement the other five Ps, so that you have every chance to be one of the success stories.

You should now understand the 6-Step Scale Up Process and be able to use it in a simple, practical way to accelerate your journey towards becoming a scale-up millionaire, regardless of the challenges you encounter along the way.

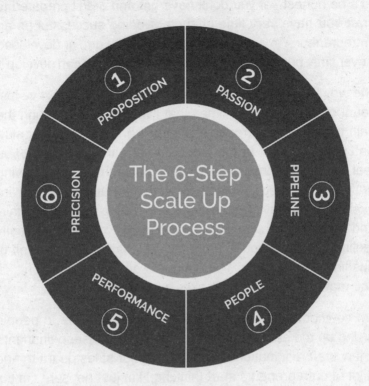

Business is tough, so tough it out

But reading about scale-up is one thing, taking action and getting results is another. One of the most important questions now is, do you have the guts, bravery, passion, determination and drive to stop thinking about it and get on with it?

And when you get knocked back and knocked down time and time again, do you think you have the resilience to get back up, keep going and fight on? Only you can answer these questions, and ultimately actions speak louder than words.

In Glasgow, we call this ability to bounce back and keep driving forward 'grit'. Aside from everything else I've said in this book, let's be honest – if you don't have grit and aren't prepared to graft you have very little chance of being successful as an entrepreneur. I'm not sure if I was born with grit, or developed it over time, but either way I'm convinced anyone can develop it.

The way I look at it, pain is a good thing in business. I've lost count of the number of times that I've had to go through the pain barrier to get through challenges and out the other side. And when you get to the other side and things go well, you feel a massive sense of satisfaction and achievement, having grafted and gritted your teeth to get there. Pain means you are pushing hard, striving, going for it, and testing yourself mentally and physically in pursuit of your dreams. If you're not currently feeling any pain, you're probably not challenging yourself or pushing hard enough. The old quote about 'what doesn't kill you makes you stronger' makes a lot of sense.

I'm convinced that most start-up failures are due to people giving up too easily. A few rejections, a few disappointments, a few staff resignations, a couple of poor sales quarters and a lot of entrepreneurs start thinking, 'I'm just not sure I'm cut out for this.' I strongly advise you not to contemplate failure at any stage. Don't become one of the quitters.

Believe me, every successful entrepreneur (including me) has felt exhausted, dejected and downbeat time after time, and the reason they've become successful is that they've managed to find a way to put their disappointments behind them (or let the negatives bounce off them) and continue on their course towards the promised land.

The fact that one of the most popular business books of all time is *The Art of War*,[1] by Chinese general Sun Tzu, says a

---

1   Sun Tzu, *The Art of War*, Seven Treasures Publications 2014.

lot about the fact that to be successful in business you need to recognise that the journey is going to be tough, testing and arduous, and that in order to succeed you will need to prepare as if you were going into battle and be able to outwit and outmanoeuvre your competition.

You've got one chance – use it

There's also a lot of talk about how many failures the most successful entrepreneurs have before becoming successful. That may or may not be the case, but the point you need to remember is that we're not trying to turn you into a billionaire or write your name in the history books as one of the most successful entrepreneurs of all time. So forget Bill Gates, Mark Zuckerberg, Elon Musk, Reid Hoffman or any of the other high profile entrepreneurs who have made personal fortunes while growing 'unicorn' businesses (businesses worth more than $1 billion). They are all geniuses and incredible entrepreneurs, but we're living in the real world, and trying to be like them is likely to send you down the wrong road and end in demotivation and disappointment. Forget about others, and focus on yourself.

Remember, our objective is merely to turn you into a successful scale-up millionaire who skilfully grows a small business and ends up with a seven or eight figure sum sitting in your personal bank account. It's a very exciting vision, definitely an achievable dream, and one that you now have the route map for.

We all know the cliché that life is short. More than halfway through my life (probably) and my business career, I'm starting to understand that. It doesn't seem that long ago that I was starting out on my career as a fresh-faced, ambitious young man.

So, if you're serious about becoming a successful entrepreneur there's no time to waste. Building an enterprise always takes longer than you expect, and you don't want to wake up in 10 or 20 years' time and think, 'OMG, why didn't I get off my butt and build that entrepreneurial business I always dreamt about?' To feel like you have missed or wasted the opportunity must be one of the worst feelings in the world!

There is also no better time to become an entrepreneur. When I started out as an entrepreneur it was seen as an unusual route to follow and there was very little support, backing, funding or digital support. Today, entrepreneurship is a respected profession, and governments, organisations, banks and business people are falling over themselves to inspire, support and back entrepreneurial people and entrepreneurial organisations. Universities now offer degrees in entrepreneurship and there are a mind-boggling number of seed camps, boot camps, tech scale-ups, tech cities, networking organisations, and a whole lot more.

So you don't really have any excuse for not getting on with it. You've got the structure, process, support mechanisms and entrepreneurial culture to get going. And you've got the chance to create something special and make a difference. Now it's up to you.

Lead with your passion

To achieve your dream scale-up, you will definitely need to use your passion to drive you forward towards your goal. I love this quote from one of Roald Dahl's books:

> *'[Uncle Oswald] taught me that if you are inter-*
> *ested in something, no matter what it is, go at it*
> *at full speed ahead. Embrace it with both arms,*
> *hug it, love it and above all become passionate*
> *about it. Lukewarm is no good. Hot is no good*

*either. White hot and passionate is the only thing
to be.'* [2]

It elegantly sums up the mindset you need to adopt as an ambitious entrepreneur if you are to convince, energise, and persuade people to buy into you, your products and your company.

As we've already established, your passion is the key tool to inspire and create interest and desire in your potential clients. Passion shouldn't be excitement at the chance to jump on a trend in order to make a quick profit. It should be about the belief in your product, the idea that it may have a positive impact on your community or the world in some way. And your passion should be enough to keep you motivated day in and day out, during all the ups and downs of growing an entrepreneurial business.

Your passion can also enable you to make those all-important high value sales when you are founder selling. Your passion can inspire prospects, clients, and your own people to believe in you, follow you and be loyal to you. And your passion should mean that you love what you're doing. And when you love what you're doing, you're going to fight hard every day to build your product and your company.

Enjoy the journey

Most entrepreneurs I've met are impatient to reach their destination, which I can understand. However, you can't reach a destination without going on a journey to get there!

We've already discussed that you will have ups and downs on this journey. But if you do it the right way (and follow the advice

---

2   Roald Dahl, *My Uncle Oswald*, Penguin 2011.

given in this book!), my experience is that you will have many more good days than bad days.

Growing a business is a serious challenge, but it can also be a lot of fun! The years ahead will be more rewarding if you enjoy the journey. Enjoy every day, enjoy all the challenges and experiences, and surround yourself with people who are positive, upbeat and want to have fun as well as work hard.

Last week, when I was on a ferry coming back from France, I bumped into an old colleague who used to work for BigHand and who I hadn't seen for more than ten years. His first comment to me was, 'Gordon, wasn't it brilliant when we used to play football in the corridor with a tennis ball?' It seemed like a strange opening remark, but it quickly reminded me what day-to-day fun we used to have! We then reminisced about all the brilliant company awaydays and weekend trips we used to have, to the Isle of Wight, Paris for Christmas dinner, boating on the Norfolk Broads, camping in Studland, skydiving in Cambridgeshire and many more. Brilliant memories, brilliant times, brilliant people – lots of fun mixed in with the blood, sweat and tears.

Know when it's time to exit

Be aware that when you get your own scale-up right, you will have a heart-wrenching decision to make at some stage about whether to keep on trucking, or whether to cash in your chips and exit. It's always a difficult (but nice) decision to make, so my only advice is not rush any huge decisions like this, but to take your time, and in the end rely mainly on your gut feeling.

If you feel that your passion and drive are starting to wane and it's feeling more like a job, that could be the moment to consider an exit (assuming the company is worth enough to give you what you feel you deserve). Some people feel they've sold too early, others feel they left it too late. Timing is everything.

Don't forget, whatever you sell for, and however much money you make personally, someone just down the road (or across the corridor) will sell tomorrow for more. So it's a question of what you are happy with and not comparing yourself with others! The key thing is that the right exit for you should give you a huge sense of pride, achievement and satisfaction that should last a lifetime.

Just do it

So that's it; I really don't have any more advice to give you. It's over to you, and up to you what you do now.

To kick-start things, I would strongly recommend you briefly go through each chapter summary and create a short set of key notes and a one-page action plan for yourself. Then have faith in your vision and start taking action today, or tomorrow at the latest. Remember, this is not rocket science, this is practical common sense and the longer you delay starting the process, the harder it will be to get going.

Becoming a scale-up millionaire is now in your own hands, and I wish you all the luck in the world in the pursuit of your entrepreneurial dreams. And finally, please let me know how you get on. Nothing will give me greater pleasure than hearing a success story from a fellow scale-up millionaire.

The Secret Millionaire

GOVAN, GLASGOW

A cold, cheerless April day turned into a dreich, drizzly, dank evening. I arrived in Govan Road at about 11pm, after a bus ride from Glasgow Central Station. The pubs were closing and locals were spilling onto the streets. I had no idea where I was going, except for a scrawled address on the handwritten post-it note I gripped tightly in my hand. I stopped outside Govan underground station and asked a guy for directions. I showed him the name of the street I was heading towards. He looked at my piece of paper and said, 'Oh no, mate, absolute shithole – that's the worst street in Govan, full of druggies! Why are you going there?' I explained that I was going to be living there for a while and he visibly winced. He gave me the directions and waved me off with a cheery 'Best of luck, pal.'

I wasn't feeling good at that stage and was wondering why I had agreed to put myself through this. Anyway, I gritted my teeth and headed off down the road. I had a guy walking behind me with a camera filming my every move as well as a guy in front of us with a big boom sound mike, and as we walked past the first pub a couple of locals shouted out, 'F*****g twats, who the f**k dae youse think you are?'

Welcome to Govan! We picked up the pace and eventually reached my residence for the next eight days. My footsteps echoed on the cold stone floor of the tenement staircase as I headed up to the apartment, unlocked the main door and had a look round my new home. The bedroom had a dirty-looking mattress on an even dirtier looking carpet. I opened one of the drawers in the dresser and found some used needles. The flat was freezing cold and I tried to switch on the boiler, but it was broken. I went into the living room and there was one sofa and no other furniture, not even a television. I looked in the kitchen cupboards and drawers, and there was nothing - not even a plate, knife and fork, or a mug.

The film crew took away my wallet and gave me an envelope containing £65, the jobseekers' allowance on which I would have to survive for the next week. They made their farewells and said they would see me at 7am the next morning, when we would start exploring the local area. Nice guys, but they were going off to stay in a nice comfy hotel while I had to stay in this 'shithole'. The front door slammed shut and I was alone, cold, and scared about the night ahead, let alone the rest of the week.

As I lay on the scraggy mattress trying to snatch some sleep, I played things over in my mind. When Channel 4 had called me out of the blue a few months before and asked me if I would like to appear on *The Secret Millionaire,* it had seemed like a good, timely opportunity. I had started to feel a bit guilty after selling our business, which I must admit is not a feeling I'd expected. But when you make some money, I think it is a natural reaction to feel a little bit guilty and selfish, even if you have worked hard for it.

Anyway, that's how I felt! For the last two years, I had been trying to work out a way of assuaging this feeling of guilt and giving something back to society. This programme had seemed like the perfect way to do so. I'd always admired this television series, as I've always felt strongly that people who are successful in life have a moral duty to help others who are less fortunate than themselves. I knew that agreeing to do this project would put me way out of my comfort zone, but I felt that might be a good thing, as my life right now seemed far too comfortable.

Anyway, I had committed to doing the programme. Where we were going was always going to be a secret. The director of my episode called me the day before we were due to start and told me I would be flying from Heathrow to Edinburgh. This sounded OK to me, as I'd always liked Edinburgh, so I boarded the flight the next day in good spirits. But when we arrived at Edinburgh Airport, we jumped into a cab that took us to Waverley train station. It was then that the director said, 'Right, Gordon, we're not staying here. We're heading through to Glasgow and you'll be spending the next eight days in Govan.' I said to him, 'You've got to be joking, right?', to which he replied, 'No, Gordon, we're not joking. We're booked on the next train to Glasgow and we need to jump on it right now.' I felt sick. Sick with fear. Sick that these guys had played a trick on me.

I'd grown up in Glasgow, but in one of the privileged areas, and had gone to a good private school. My dad had grown up near Govan in the days when it had a proud and booming ship-building industry – when Billy Connolly was a welder at one of the big shipyards! But I also knew that the demise of ship-building and the related heavy industry meant that Govan had fallen on brutally hard times over the past few decades. And a guy from a posh part of Glasgow who had been softened up even further through many years in the south of England was now heading there.

When I woke up the next morning in my cold, cheerless Govan flat, I experienced a strange surge of optimism as I realised that against all odds I had got some sleep, was still alive, and actually felt as if things could only get better!

After I'd had a cold shower, the film crew arrived and explained the rules of engagement: I would be living a 'secret' life for the next eight days. I would live like one of the locals, in the same basic accommodation, with the same money in my pocket and like most of them I would be unemployed. The crew had been in the local area for a couple of weeks beforehand, creating a 'cover' story that they were filming a brand new series for Channel 4 about guys like me who had left their home towns many years before to make their way in the world and then had come back for a visit to see what had changed.

The film crew and the director, Kevin, would follow me with the cameras wherever I wanted to go. Absolutely no one was to know who I was, or that I was a successful entrepreneur. During my time here, my objective was to integrate myself into the community and identify charity organisations that deserved some financial help from me. On the last day, all being well, I would reveal my true identity and give away some of my own money.

So off we went! I was starving hungry, so we headed down Govan High Street and I asked directions to the local café. We turned up at one of Govan's favourite cafés, Gaynor's, and I sat down feeling a little nervous about the questions people might ask. The first question was, 'So what's all this about with the film crew?' I gave the pre-rehearsed answer about the new series that I would repeat many times, and they seemed to accept it. Phew! I relaxed a little. As I was munching my way through a delicious 'full Scottish' breakfast, Gaynor's father asked me a bit about myself. I lied again (it felt horrible but I would soon get used to it) and told him that I had been made redundant from the pharmaceutical company that I worked for. He seemed genuinely concerned about this and when I came to pay, he said, 'Dinnae be ridiculous, sonny, this one is on the hoose. Sounds like you need all the money you've got right now.'

I couldn't believe the kindness – if only he knew. Anyway, I thanked him graciously and headed off feeling uplifted at just how friendly they had been. It made me remember that it doesn't matter how poor a community is, life is all about people and there are good people everywhere. At that stage, I felt determined to do all I could to help this community.

I spent the next eight days trudging the streets, chatting to people, asking questions about where the local volunteer charities were based. My feelings of fear and dread at surviving in this seemingly desolate community soon disappeared. I realised I needed to stop thinking selfishly about myself – it wasn't about me, it was about the people who lived here. I would be leaving in a week's time and they would have to stay.

I met some great characters. I met families where the son was third generation unemployed: he, his father and his grandfather, would all be sitting in the same room, and they had never ever worked. But I can tell you, they still had the banter and the best sense of humour. Every day that went by I got more excited about the fact that soon I was actually going to be able to help.

I met some great volunteer organisations and through doing some volunteer work myself, I also managed to get myself a brand-new duvet and some crockery and cutlery for my flat. I felt I was starting to build a bit of a life for myself in this community.

Two charities in particular took me under their wings: Sunny Govan Community Radio and Galgael. Sunny Govan had a brilliant team of people, including Heather and Jim and their brilliantly talented head DJ, Steg G, who interviewed me live on air several times! They accepted any youngster who walked in off the streets and taught them the art of DJ-ing and MC-ing. They gave them confidence and something to dream about. They taught them about manners and respect.

Galgael would welcome anyone in who wanted to come. They taught people the art of using their hands and working skilfully with wood. They would start with small wooden carvings and make their way up to building full-sized galley boats, which they would row and sail up the River Clyde and beyond. Galgael is an incredible charity that I personally found hugely inspiring.

What astonished me about these charities is that volunteers worked there incredibly hard, but walked away at the end of the week with no pay cheque, no money. The team spirit, the dedication, the commitment, the professionalism - they would put a lot of businesses and fully paid employees to shame. And they earned nothing! They did it because they couldn't find any jobs and they wanted to help out, rather than sitting around at home.

What a brilliant attitude! What inspirational people! Whenever I'm feeling slightly downbeat, lazy or lethargic about work or life, I think of these guys and it quickly resets my attitude.

Every so often I would feel the fear again and witness aggressive and violent behaviour. One Saturday night, when I was outside the Sunny Govan headquarters, a couple of guys outside the pub started threatening us viciously. But I soon realised this was the exception rather than the rule and that you just had to let it bounce off you, hold your head high, walk away and focus on the positives.

Before I realised it, my eight-day visit was nearing its end. I started to get a little sad, as I genuinely didn't want to leave. I was learning so much, meeting such great people, opening my eyes, and also realising how lucky I was in the life that I led. But I knew that I had to leave; my time was up.

On my last night, I felt very upbeat as I sat in my wee flat and started to write some cheques to the charities I wanted to help. I put my pen down; the decisions were made. I had written cheques totalling £50,000. It felt great! I was so excited about tomorrow.

I woke up after a great night's sleep feeling energised. The good people of Govan had been very kind to me and now it was time for me to repay their kindness.

Tam from Galgael called the whole workshop together – about 50 guys. He explained that it was my last day and they'd really enjoyed working with me, so they'd like to present me with a Galgael T-shirt. Everyone cheered and clapped. I was touched. Now it was my turn. I explained that I'd had to be a bit secretive over the last week but that I had been fortunate in business and the reality was that we had been filming *The Secret Millionaire*. I was their secret millionaire and I wanted to give them a cheque to buy a rescue rib boat with. I knew from working with them that they wanted this badly, as when they went out in their wooden boats they really needed a rescue boat alongside. There was silence, then whooping, cheering, and clapping. Everyone was coming up and shaking my hand, hugging me and thanking me from the bottom of their hearts. It was very emotional for all of us, for different reasons. I could tell this donation would make a huge difference.

Next stop, Sunny Govan. I asked for a private meeting with the founder, Heather, in one of the offices. I explained my secret and how I would like to help financially. She broke down in tears and said, 'Gordon, dreams can come true, dreams can come true!' My own eyes welled up as we went through to the main office to meet the rest of the team and for Heather to make an announcement. Same as at Galgael – incredible joy, backslapping and gratitude.

Steg G uttered the final profound words of my memorable stay in Govan: 'Gordon, you've touched not only us, but people in the wider community, people whose faces you will never see, and we can't thank you enough for that.'

I later found out that Sunny Govan were literally on the verge of going bankrupt before my cheque arrived. At the time of writing, they have gone from strength to strength. The money gave them a lifeline and the confidence to stay true to their vision.

The *Secret Millionaire* experience completed my circle. If you can be successful in scaling up an entrepreneurial business, I guarantee you that giving some of your money away and personally supporting charitable organisations in a way that makes a real difference will be the most rewarding bit, by far.

Hoping I can continue to make a difference in the future is what keeps me pushing on in business and in life.

Acknowledgements

I'm a lucky man with a good life, but I certainly wouldn't have been able to gain the expertise and experience to write this book without all the advice, support and encouragement from many, many people throughout the course of my career to date.

I can only name a handful of these people here now, but also want to thank each and every person who has helped me along the way - you know who you are!

Firstly, I'd like to thank my first 'big boss' at Astra Zeneca, Chris Corbin, who set me on the right career path by believing in me and igniting my belief that I could be successful at sales.

I was extremely lucky to have such a talented co-founder at BigHand, Steve Thompson, who ran the business superbly and released my sales team and I to fly, so huge thanks to Steve for an unforgettable ten-year journey together. Thanks also to Chris White, a client, colleague and friend who has been 100% positive about everything I've done over the last 20 years.

My Dad is a proud man with a fierce work ethos and it's him I need to thank for teaching me that you get nothing in life without hard graft, focus and dedication, while still remembering to keep your feet on the ground. My late Mum always believed in my dreams and it's her I want to thank for instilling in me a burning desire to make a real difference in this world, without ever forgetting others who may be less fortunate.

My in-laws, John (retired fellow sales person) and Jen also deserve special thanks for their unconditional, unstinting encouragement and support, when others may have advised me to go and get a 'real job'.

Finally, my wonderful wife Claire met me when I didn't really have all that much, except 'potential', and has backed and supported me patiently through all the challenges of an entrepreneurial life. She's also a great mum to our two girls Mia and Holly, who continually remind me what life is really all about and make me a proud dad each and every day.

If you've enjoyed *Scale Up Millionaire* it would mean a lot to Gordon if you could go to amazon.co.uk and take a couple of minutes to provide a quick review:

To submit an Amazon review:

» Type 'Scale Up Millionaire' in search box at top of the home page

» Click on book image to go to the product details page for *Scale Up Millionaire* on Amazon.co.uk. (then scroll half way down this page to reach Customer Reviews)

» Click on 'Write a customer review' button in Customer Reviews section.

» Rate the book and write your review.

» Click Submit.

Also visit www.gordonmcalpine.co.uk to see details of services including:

» Scale Up Healthcheck – FREE assessment of the scale up health of your enterprise and key actions you can take to improve

» GM Advisory Services – APPLY to become part of an elite group of fast growth, entrepreneurial businesses who receive advice, support and mentoring personally from Gordon McAlpine

» Keynote Speaking – MOTIVATIONAL keynote speaking for your sales conferences, team building events and inspirational client events

» Blog – regular thought leadership updates on the GM blog

Web: www.gordonmcalpine.co.uk
Twitter: @GordonMcAlpine
LinkedIn: https://uk.linkedin.com/in/gordonmcalpine

The Author

Gordon McAlpine has worked in sales for more than two decades and has been an entrepreneur for most of that time. He was born and raised in Glasgow, Scotland and now lives in rural Berkshire with his wife and family.

He was educated at Kelvinside Academy, Glasgow and went on to complete an MA in Economics & Accountancy at The University of Aberdeen and an M.Sc in Marketing at The University of Strathclyde Business School.

After a stellar five-year start to his sales career at pharmaceutical giant Astra Zeneca, he co-founded technology start-up BigHand from his living room, and as Sales & Marketing Director was responsible for driving the global Scale Up to successful exit, without ever receiving any funding from investors or the bank.

In 2010, he appeared on Channel 4's *The Secret Millionaire* TV programme, visiting Govan in Glasgow, a proud community which has fallen on hard times since the decline of the shipbuilding industry. He lived 'under cover' in local social housing for eight days and ended up giving away tens of thousands of pounds of his own money to local charities.

Gordon also founded (and exited) the world's first membership club for sales leaders, The Sales Club, which as a sales centre of excellence provided ideas, inspiration, innovation and best practice benchmarking to many of the world's leading companies to help them improve the sales performance of their sales teams.

Gordon is now focused on the booming British technology space, personally advising fast-growth entrepreneurial organisations on how to scale up through sales. As a Business Fellow at Strathclyde University Business School, and a Tech London Advocate, he's also involved in inspiring and mentoring the rising stars of UK Entrepreneurship.

Twitter: @GordonMcAlpine
LinkedIn: https://uk.linkedin.com/in/gordonmcalpine
Web: www.gordonmcalpine.co.uk